Nutshell Series

Federal Courts

in a nutshell®

DAVID P. CURRIE
DONALD L. DOERNBERG

5TH EDITION

FEDERAL COURTS

IN A NUTSHELL®

FIFTH EDITION

DAVID P. CURRIE
Late Edward H. Levi Distinguished
Service Professor
The Law School
The University of Chicago

DONALD L. DOERNBERG
Professor of Law
Pace University School of Law

**WEST
ACADEMIC**
PUBLISHING

TABLE OF CONTENTS

PREFACE

West designed the Nutshell series as "succinct exposition[s] of the law to which a student or lawyer can turn for reliable guidance." The critical word is "guidance." A Nutshell cannot be more than a guide, highlighting law that is relatively clearly established and areas where unsettled questions abound, with suggested approaches. Bear those limitations in mind when using any Nutshell.

I have often told my Federal Courts students that it is not possible to simplify the doctrine of Federal Courts. It is only possible to oversimplify it. I hope that the following pages will do a reasonable job of summarizing areas where the law is clear and offering ways to think about the areas in which it is not.

Law does not fit into neat compartments, and that affects all nutshells. For example, the availability of post-conviction remedies has much to do with how the federal courts function institutionally *vis-à-vis* Congress and the states. But post-conviction remedies can be (and in many schools is) a course unto itself. Although, I have tried to separate considerations relating to federal-courts doctrine from those fitting better in a post-conviction-remedies course, the line between them is fuzzy and constantly shifting.

Refer again to the caution from the first paragraph above.

The organization of this volume differs from that of its predecessors in two major ways. First, many Civil Procedure and Federal Courts books treat removal as a kind of jurisdiction somehow different from the "ordinary" subject-matter jurisdiction categories—federal-question jurisdiction and diversity jurisdiction. But it is not; it simply is a manner of *invoking* federal jurisdiction that Congress established elsewhere in various sections of Title 28, most notably in §§ 1331 (federal question), 1332 (diversity), 1333 (admiralty), 1334 (bankruptcy) and 1338 (copyrights, patents, trademarks). There is no separate category of "removal jurisdiction."

Second, many books treat the abstention doctrines as a major subject apart from subject-matter jurisdiction. Conceptually, it makes more sense to treat those doctrines as a subcategory of a more general discussion of subject-matter jurisdiction. Typically, discussions of subject-matter jurisdiction focus on (1) the areas in which the federal courts have (sometimes exclusive) jurisdiction, (2) the limitations on that jurisdiction, and (3) areas over which the federal courts have no subject-matter jurisdiction. The abstention doctrines, for all of their complexity, are simply a fourth area, dealing with situations in which the federal courts clearly *have* subject-matter jurisdiction but refuse to exercise it.

I have used some editing conventions to keep this book to manageable size. It is *not* an exhaustive discussion—or even mention—of all of the Supreme Court cases relevant to an area. When the source of a quotation is obvious from context, I have not included a separate footnote, contrary to the dictates of both common law-review practice and the Bluebook. Similarly, I have not included second or subsequent full citations of cases, despite the Bluebook's demands. (I am especially proud of not wasting the time and space that slavish adherence to the Bluebook requires.)

When context calls for a singular pronoun, I have used "he" and "she" randomly; unless the pronoun refers to an identified party to a case, it is not intended to be sex-specific. (I just cannot bring myself to use "they" as a substitute for the singular pronoun, even though it may be more politically correct. It still is not good writing.)

D.L.D.

TABLE OF CASES

FEDERAL COURTS

IN A NUTSHELL®

FIFTH EDITION

INTRODUCTION

The United States is a unified nation for some purposes but not others. It has more than fifty components—states, territories and the District of Columbia—each of which has its own governmental system, and the fifty states have areas of power into which the federal government may not intrude. By the same token, the federal government has areas of power exempt from interference from the states. If all those areas were clearly defined, life under our legal system would be much simpler. But they are not. There are many areas in which federal and non-federal power overlap and operate concurrently.

The Constitutional Law course directly concerns the fuzzy boundaries among areas of exclusive federal power, exclusive state power, and concurrent governmental powers, under the rubric of federalism. That is not the only complexity; within each level of government, the different branches—legislative, executive, and judicial—each have powers. Some of those powers are exclusive to one branch, but others are shared. That defines another theme: separation of powers.

The course in Federal Courts concerns the institutional role of the federal court system in elaborating those two themes: federalism and separation of powers. The federal courts have enormous power, but in sharply limited areas. Understanding the federal courts' relationships with state governments (especially state judiciaries) and with the other branches of the federal government requires grappling with doctrines that have developed to deal with the complexities of inter-system and inter-branch relationships. The Constitutional Convention had to confront at least four major areas of conflict. The first, thrust on the Convention by the failure of the Articles of Confederation to provide a workable national structure, regards the balance of power between the central government and the states—federalism. The second involves the distribution of power within the new government—separation of powers. For the fifty-five delegates at the Convention, the challenge was to evolve a structural plan that would address both areas. That involved much discussion, debate, and compromise, and the product that eventually emerged is the main body of the Constitution.

There were two other major areas of concern at the Convention, and they were closely related. One was whether the Constitution should provide direct protection for individual rights. No one seriously questioned that there were areas of concern to individuals into which the central government could not properly intrude. The sticking point was the concern that by enumerating some rights in the Constitution, the Convention might seem to be excluding by implication rights not enumerated—the familiar *expressio-unius-est-exclusio-alterius* maxim of construction.[1] The last area involved slavery, an area linked to individual rights because it concerned the question of whom the Constitution should recognize as "persons." The Convention dealt with those issues in a way now all too familiar to observers of recent Congresses: it kicked the cans down the road. As for slavery, the Constitution (art. I, § 9, cl. 1) created a twenty-year moratorium on federal action to prevent importation of slaves (whom, curiously, that clause *does* recognize as persons), setting the stage for the ongoing battle over "race" relations, now more than two centuries old.

The delegates did not include provisions about individual rights, leaving the issue to the amendment process. There was a general understanding that the first Congress would address those issues, and it did. Several states ratified the Constitution on the explicit understanding that a Bill of Rights would follow.

---

[1] That concern led to the Ninth Amendment, which warns against the inference.

I. FEDERAL COURT STRUCTURE

A.   Article III Courts and Judges

The Constitution created only the United States Supreme Court. The Convention debated whether should be any other federal courts. So, as it had with individual rights and slavery, the Convention deferred resolution to Congress when Article III, § 1, provided that there would be "one supreme Court, and * * * such inferior Courts as the Congress may from time to time ordain and establish." The battle over inferior federal courts at the Convention pitted the Federalists against the Anti-Federalists. When the Federalists won a majority in the new Congress, they wasted no time in establishing a system of inferior federal courts. All federal judgeships Congress creates under Article III have the constitutional protections of service "during good Behaviour" (now generally understood to be for life unless a judge is convicted of a crime, in which case impeachment may follow) and salaries that Congress cannot reduce during a judge's tenure.

The system Congress established, however, was not the three-tier system with which you are familiar. There were three kinds of federal courts (with the Supreme Court at the top), but the inferior courts' jurisdiction differed radically from today's model. Congress created two types of trial courts, known as district courts and circuit courts. District courts were exclusively courts of original jurisdiction. They served as trial courts principally in maritime cases and in the prosecution of minor federal crimes. Originally there were thirteen districts, divided essentially along state lines.

There were three circuit courts composed of two Supreme Court Justices and the local district judge, and each incorporating several district courts. The circuit courts had both original and appellate functions. They reviewed decisions of the district courts, and they were also the trial courts for diversity cases and for major government litigation. Neither the district nor the circuit courts had general jurisdiction over cases arising under federal law.

B. Article I Courts and Judges

Article I courts, known colloquially as legislative courts, got their start in 1828. The Florida territorial legislature created a territorial court. The question arose whether the judges of that court were entitled to the protections of Article III judges. The Supreme Court found that the Florida court derived from Congress's Article IV, § 3, cl. 2, power to govern territories, not from Article III. Therefore, the Article III protections did not apply.

Later cases extended this principle to military courts, consular courts in foreign countries, and, more recently, local courts in the District of Columbia. All these instances involved extraordinary situations. It is plausible that the Framers did not intend to burden the system with additional judges enjoying unlimited tenure during good behavior. Article I courts, therefore, operate under the real or imagined shadow of direct congressional oversight, a situation against which the Framers carefully guarded in Article III. Chapter II(B) discusses Article I courts at greater length.

II. THE COURTS AND THE CONSTITUTION

A. Justiciability

Article III extends the judicial power only to specified types of "cases" and "controversies," and the Supreme Court has made clear that Article III courts cannot hear matters not qualifying as "cases" or "controversies." The Case-or-Controversy Clause embraces several limitations on the federal courts' authority.

1. Finality

The courts will not act if their decisions are subject to executive or legislative review. In *Hayburn's Case*,[2] five Justices sitting on circuit refused to adjudicate veterans' pension claims because the statute allowed the Secretary of War to disregard their findings if he discovered imposition or mistake. The finality limitation may be a corollary of Article III's guarantees of tenure during good behavior and irreducible salary. If, as Hamilton said in the Federalist, Article III insulates the process of decision from executive or legislative influence, executive power to set aside a judicial decision is intolerable. On the other hand, perhaps the guarantees are only insulation for federal judges' on-going decision-making process—guarantees against personal retaliation—rather than forbidding further ac-

---

[2] 2 U.S. (2 Dall.) 408 (1792).

tion after the judicial process in the Article III courts has concluded. Be that as it may, the federal courts scrupulously protect *Hayburn's Case*'s principle.

But finality is one thing; efficacy is another. Congress can frustrate a money judgment against the United States by refusing to appropriate money to pay it, and any other federal judgment is ineffective if the executive fails to enforce it.[3] Probably for this reason, one well known commentator termed finality the least important element of the case-or-controversy requirement.

2. Advisory Opinions

In Massachusetts (and perhaps other states) and Canada, the courts will give advice to the executive or to the legislature on important public questions. The United States' federal courts will not. In 1793, at President Washington's request, Secretary of State Jefferson asked the Justices their opinions on a number of abstract legal questions respecting American neutrality in the ongoing war between England and

---

[3] Congress and the President cannot, however, *undo* a case that has proceeded to final judgment, even if that judgment rests on misunderstanding Congress's intent. Plaut v. Spendthrift Farm, Inc., 514 U.S. 211 (1995).

France. In a letter to Jefferson, the Justices declined to answer.

There is something to be said for advisory opinions. They avoid the delays and uncertainties of ordinary litigation and facilitate judicial review. But advisory opinions have disadvantages as well. Concrete facts help a court to understand the likely import of its decision; adverse parties help to ensure that the court has both sides of the question before it. Abstract pronouncements on questions of law may create unnecessary conflict with other branches. Judicial lawmaking is easiest to reconcile with democratic theory when it is the inevitable byproduct of deciding individual disputes. Time spent resolving abstract questions may distract judges from that more central function. The modern explanation is that a request for an advisory opinion does not present a case or controversy within the meaning of Article III.

A related question is whether the majoritarian branches may ask judges to step off the Bench to perform nonjudicial duties. Two early Chief Justices were sent to negotiate treaties with foreign nations. Justice Jackson took a year off to prosecute war criminals at Nuremberg. Chief Justice Warren led the investigation of President Kennedy's assassination.

There are at least three kinds of objections to such activity: (1) the loss of time to devote to judicial tasks, (2) the risk of controversy that might impair public confidence in judicial decisions, and (3) the danger that judges might be tempted to render decisions that will please the executive in order to attract desirable assignments. Nevertheless, *Mistretta v. United States*[4] held that federal judges could constitutionally sit on a commission to draft sentencing guidelines for criminal cases. History showed that the Constitution "does not forbid judges from wearing two hats; it merely forbids them from wearing both hats at the same time."

3. Standing

Standing—the question of whether the litigant is the proper party to assert a claim or argument—could easily be a book by itself, so tortured is the Court's jurisprudence. Keep that in mind, because a nutshell can present only the broad outlines of the Court's doctrine, necessarily glossing over its many nuances. Questions of standing ordinarily arise when a litigant challenges some government action.[5]

---

[4] 488 U.S. 361 (1989).

[5] Most commonly, plaintiffs challenging governmental agency action rely on § 10(a) of the Administrative Procedure Act, 5 U.S.C. § 702: "A person suffering legal wrong because of agency action, or adversely affected or aggrieved by agency ac-

There are three constitutional requirements for standing:[6]   (1) the litigant must have suffered injury-in-fact—some harm peculiar to the litigant rather than the population generally; (2) the litigant's damage must be traceable to the challenged action, and (3) the judgment the litigant seeks must be able to redress the harm suffered.   Each prong of the constitutional test presents problems, and commentators criticize the latter two requirements as infinitely malleable at the hands of the Justices.

The Court used to have a two-level inquiry relating to standing. In addition to the constitutional *minima*, the Court imposed certain "prudential" requirements on standing.   Such requirements may still exist for cases in which Congress has not created a specific cause of action, but *Lexmark International, Inc. v. Static Control Components, Inc.*[7] held that imposing prudential requirements when Congress *has* created a cause of action violates separation of powers.

---

tion within the meaning of a relevant statute, is entitled to judicial review thereof." The statute's language merely begs the question of what constitutes a "legal wrong."

[6] Allen v. Wright, 468 U.S. 737 (1984).

[7] 134 S. Ct. 1377 (2014).

a. Injury-in-Fact

"The Article III judicial power exists only to redress or otherwise to protect against injury to the complaining party."[8] A litigant may challenge government action either because she suffers some legal wrong within the meaning of the Administrative Procedure Act (APA) or because the injury of which she complains is within the "zone of interests" a statute protects.[9] A litigant who does not "stand to profit in some personal interest"[10] by prevailing has not presented a case or controversy; he lacks standing to challenge government action. One finds the same minimum requirement of injury in numerous statutes conferring the right to challenge federal administrative action. For ex-

---

[8] Warth v. Seldin, 422 U.S. 490, 499 (1975).

[9] Clarke v. Securities Indus. Ass'n, 479 U.S. 388, 396-97 (1987), offered an example of a potential litigant who might suffer actual injury—monetary loss—but would not fall within the underlying statute's zone of interest.

> [T]he failure of an agency to comply with a statutory provision requiring "on the record" hearings would assuredly have an adverse effect upon the company that has the contract to record and transcribe the agency's proceedings; but since the provision was obviously enacted to protect the interests of the parties to the proceedings and not those of the reporters, that company would not be "adversely affected within the meaning" of the statute.

[10] Simon v. E. Kentucky Welfare Rights Org., 426 U.S. 26, 39 (1976).

ample, the APA authorizes judicial review at the behest of a person "adversely affected or aggrieved by agency action within the meaning of a relevant statute * * * ."[11]   Standing in this sense is no artificial restriction of constitutional litigation.   I cannot sue for a trespass on my neighbor's land or for negligence that injures my neighbor but not me.   In terms of the policies of the case-or-controversy requirement, a litigant needs a "personal stake in the outcome" in order to "assure that concrete adverseness which sharpens the presentation of issues * * * ."

It is not always easy to determine what constitutes adequate injury under the Constitution or the APA.   In language equally applicable to the constitutional question, *Sierra Club v. Morton*[12] held that a mere "value preference" or "intellectual interest in the problem" of conservation did not suffice under the statute.   The Club could not challenge the development of a ski resort on wilderness land without alleging that its members used the area.[13]   On the other hand,

---

[11] 5 U.S.C. § 702.

[12] 405 U.S. 727 (1972).

[13] Justice Byron White is reputed to have said, "Why didn't the Sierra Club have one goddamn member walk through the park and then there would have been standing to sue?" BOB WOODWARD & SCOTT ARMSTRONG, THE BRETHREN 164 n.* (1979).

United States v. SCRAP[14] allowed park users to attack a rate decision of the Interstate Commerce Commission by alleging that it would discourage transportation of recycled materials and thus damage the parks through extraction of raw materials and disposal of refuse. The Court said it was no ground for objection that the alleged injury was aesthetic rather than economic, that it might not be substantial, or that many other people shared it.

But the Court has scrapped *SCRAP*. *Lujan v. National Wildlife Federation*[15] characterized *SCRAP* as an expansive view of standing that the Court "has never since * * * emulated * * * ." Chief Justice Roberts later called *SCRAP* "the previous high-water mark of diluted standing requirements."   Instead, individual litigants must now show that they personally have suffered some specific loss—not that they may suffer some loss at an undefined future time by, for example, planning to visit an area they claim agency action adversely affects.

Injuries the populace as a whole suffers do not to confer standing on anyone.   The Court characterizes such cases as "generalized grievances" and denies they create injury-in-fact.   For

---

14 412 U.S. 669 (1973).

15 497 U.S. 871 (1990).

example, during the Vietnam war there were numerous challenges to the war's legality; the Court invariably found no standing. "The assumption that if respondents have no standing to sue, no one would have standing, is not a reason to find standing."[16]

b. Traceability and Redressability

Traceability is causation "looking backward." Redressability is causation "looking forward." With respect to traceability, claimants must—as in every claim in every area of the law—show that the opposing party caused the harm that the claimants allege. Claimants must also show that winning would stop (or at least ameliorate) the injury-in-fact that they claim to suffer. Thus, plaintiffs unable to pay for hospital services had no standing to challenge the hospital's charitable tax exemption because they were unable to show that removing the exemption would cause the hospital to begin to offer services to the poor.[17] Similarly, a mother seeking to declare a Texas criminal statute that allowed prosecution of non-supporting parents only if the child was "legitimate" unconstitutional lacked standing because the Court thought it too specu-

---

[16] Schlesinger v. Reservists Comm. to Stop the War, 418 U.S. 208, 227 (1974)

[17] *Simon v. E. Kentucky* (1976).

lative that prosecuting and jailing the father would result in increased payments to the mother.[18]

4. Ripeness

The Case-or-Controversy Clause also requires that the matter be "ripe" for decision. Ripeness is a problem of prematurity. Standing concerns whether the plaintiff is the right person to bring the action; ripeness addresses whether it is the right time to bring the action. Concrete facts that would help the Court make a well-informed decision are often missing. It may not be certain what is going to happen, or even whether anything is going to happen that would create a concrete controversy. Deciding an unripe case may waste of the court's time and result in unnecessary confrontation with another branch of government.[19] A decision might turn out to have been merely advisory.

The Supreme Court's understandable reluctance to decide hypothetical cases can cause serious hardship. *United Public Workers v. Mitch-*

---

[18] Linda R.S. v. Richard D., 410 U.S. 614 (1973).

[19] It may not even be clear that the parties have anything at stake and therefore that they will present the case adequately. Ripeness thus may tend to merge with standing: because no dispute may actually develop, it may turn out that the plaintiffs are not the right parties to make a claim.

ell[20] refused to allow government employees to attack the Hatch Act, which restricted their political activities. The precise nature of their intended activities was unclear, and there was "no threat" of interference "beyond that implied by the existence of the law and the regulations." In *International Longshoremen's Union v. Boyd*,[21] resident aliens intending to do summer work in Alaska could not challenge the government's decision to subject them to the stringent requirements for new immigrants upon their return. *Poe v. Ullman*[22] disallowed an attack on a Connecticut birth-control statute on the ground that prosecutorial inertia demonstrated there was no substantial threat that the law would be enforced.

Query what options such potential plaintiffs have. The Court seemed to say that someone could only test the validity of a statute by violating it, risking punishment if the court rejected the claim. In effect, the Court was telling the citizen that "the only way to determine whether the suspect is a mushroom or a toadstool is to eat it." Congress intended the Declaratory

---

[20] 330 U.S. 75 (1947).

[21] 347 U.S. 222 (1954).

[22] 367 U.S. 497 (1961).

Judgment Act to avoid precisely this kind of risk.

Even older decisions, however, did not always require that a litigant violate the law to test it. In *Village of Euclid v. Ambler Realty Co.*,[23] an attack on a zoning ordinance was ripe because the mere existence of the ordinance reduced the property value; the land owner thus did not have to violate the ordinance to create injury-in-fact. *Adler v. Board of Education*[24] allowed a teacher to challenge the validity of a law requiring dismissal of teachers who advocated overthrow of the government, although he did not allege that he had done or intended to do what the statute forbade. And in the *Railroad Transfer* case,[25] which seems to have gone too far, the Court allowed an attack on a Chicago ordinance requiring a company to keep its principal place of business within the city, even though there was no allegation that the company contemplated moving.

More recently, the Court has explicitly recognized that the risk of enforcement of a provision of debatable validity may constrain people

[23] 272 U.S. 365 (1926).

[24] 342 U.S. 485 (1952).

[25] Railroad Transfer Service, Inc. v. City of Chicago, 386 U.S. 351 (1967).

sufficiently to create a ripe controversy. In *Roe v. Wade*,[26] a pregnant woman could attack a statute forbidding abortion; *Abbott Laboratories v. Gardner*[27] allowed a drug manufacturer to challenge a labeling requirement that the government had not yet enforced.

But the Court has been careful to open the door only to cases that present true hardships. It is unpredictable where the Justices will draw the line between real and speculative controversies. A companion case to *Abbott* held unripe a challenge to a regulation that it read to impose "no irremediable adverse consequences" in the event of a later dispute.[28] The lower courts, following this lead, refused to determine the validity of proposed regulations.[29] And in *Roe*, the Court dismissed as "speculative" the challenge of a non-pregnant woman who alleged that uncertainty as to her ability to obtain an abortion interfered with her marriage.

The degree of ripeness necessary for an informed decision may relate to a judge's views on the merits. In *Adler*, for example, a judge who believed that the state could never condition

---

[26] 410 U.S. 113 (1973).

[27] 387 U.S. 136 (1967).

[28] Toilet Goods Ass'n v. Gardner, 387 U.S. 136 (1967).

[29] Lever Bros. v. FTC, 325 F. Supp. 371 (D. Me. 1971).

employment on surrender of constitutional rights would need a less complete record than Justice Frankfurter, who thought the validity of the statute's application depended upon what the individual teacher might actually say. This reemphasizes the difference between a facial and an as-applied attack.

Ripeness relates to equitable considerations of irreparable harm that inform the traditional decision of whether injunctive relief is appropriate. It also relates to the notion that declaratory relief is discretionary, and to the principle requiring exhaustion of administrative remedies. It has both constitutional and prudential dimensions.

5. Mootness

In moot cases, the facts have already happened; there is no lack of concreteness. But the decision no longer matters; it will not change the parties' situation. Deciding such a case would present the same three issues that deciding an unripe case does. Mootness often arises after filing, and the courts will dismiss a case or vacate a judgment that becomes moot at any time before final appellate decision.

The problem, of course, is to decide when a case is moot. *Carafas v. LaVallee*[30] held that the continuing disabilities the law attaches to a felon kept a controversy over his conviction alive even after his unconditional release from prison. *United States v. W.T. Grant Co.*[31] stated an important limitation on the mootness doctrine: a case does not become moot simply because the challenged behavior has ceased if there is a substantial likelihood that it will be resumed.

In the past few decades, the Supreme Court has created an exception to the ordinary mootness doctrine. In *Roe v. Wade*, for example, a plaintiff seeking a declaration of her right to an abortion was pregnant when she sued but had given birth when the case reached the Supreme Court. To hold the case moot, the Court said, would effectively prevent judicial review of abortion questions because of the short period between conception and birth; the issue was "capable of repetition, yet evading review." When time constraints would effectively insulate a law from judicial scrutiny, the Court's policy is understandable, but it is difficult to see how the unavailability of normal review makes the mat-

---

[30] 391 U.S. 234 (1968).

[31] 345 U.S. 629 (1953).

ter any less moot, or any more a constitutional "controversy."

Class actions have further eroded the mootness doctrine. *Sosna v. Iowa*[32] applied the "evading review" exception to a class action challenge to a residency requirement the representative plaintiff had satisfied during litigation. Initially the Court limited the authority of the mooted representative to cases in which the trial court had already certified the class. In two 1980 decisions, however, the Court allowed plaintiffs' appeal from refusal to certify a class, although their individual claims were by then moot.[33] In the second case, the named plaintiffs had received an offer of the full amount of their individual claims in settlement. They retained an interest "in their desire to shift part of the costs of litigation to those who will share in its benefits if the class is certified."

6. Political Questions

The Court shies from cases it thinks present only "political" questions. *Luther v. Borden*[34] refused to determine which of two competing bodies was the legitimate government of Rhode Is-

---

[32] 419 U.S. 393 (1975)

[33] United States Parole Comm'n v. Geraghty, 445 U.S. 388 (1980); Deposit Guar. Nat'l Bank v. Roper, 445 U.S. 326 (1980).

[34] 48 U.S. (7 How.) 1 (1849).

land, rejecting the argument that the Guaranty Clause of Article IV provided a basis for adjudication. *Pacific States Tel. Co. v. Oregon*[35] refused to decide whether a state might constitutionally adopt legislation by initiative or referendum. *Colegrove v. Green*[36] refused to determine the constitutionality of unequal apportionment of congressional seats. The reason *Luther* and *Pacific States* gave and that Justice Frankfurter's opinion in *Colegrove* echoed was that the issues were "political," not judicial.

Baker v. Carr[37] made a critical change. It upheld a federal court's authority to determine the constitutionality of electoral districts for state legislators, distinguishing *Colegrove*. *Baker* rested on the Equal Protection Clause, not the Guaranty Clause. The Court noted that the political-question doctrine is a function of federal separation of powers, not federalism.

> Prominent on the surface of any case held to involve a political question is found [1] a textually demonstrable constitutional commitment of the issue to a coordinate political department; or [2] a lack of judicially discoverable and

---

[35] 223 U.S. 118 (1912).

[36] 328 U.S. 549 (1946).

[37] 369 U.S. 186 (1962).

manageable standards for resolving it; or [3] the impossibility of deciding without an initial policy determination of a kind clearly for nonjudicial discretion; or [4] the impossibility of a court's undertaking independent resolution without expressing lack of the respect due coordinate branches of government; or [5] an unusual need for unquestioning adherence to a political decision already made; or [6] the potentiality of embarrassment from multifarious pronouncements by various departments on one question * * * .

The Court found that *Baker* had none of these characteristics.

Powell v. McCormack[38] appeared to erode the political-question doctrine to some extent. The Court upheld judicial authority to pass upon the exclusion of an elected Congressman. A strong majority held that Article I's provision making each House "Judge of the * * * Qualifications of its own Members," committed to Congress only the power to determine whether a member met constitutional requirements of age, citizenship, and residence, not to deny membership for alleged misuse of House funds. The

---

[38] 395 U.S. 486 (1969).

Court rapidly downplayed the fourth and sixth *Baker* criteria; adjudicating would demonstrate no "lack of respect" for other branches, since it required only the traditional judicial exercise of interpreting the Constitution. Nor would it result in "multifarious pronouncements * * * on one question," since the Court's word was law.

The Court continues to invoke the doctrine, however.   *O'Brien v. Brown*[39] stayed enforcement of a lower-court decision respecting seating delegates to the 1972 Democratic National Convention.   In weighing the public-interest and probability-of-success criteria relevant to the stay question, however, the Court strongly suggested the ultimate issue was "political."   Another case found that the question whether the President could terminate a treaty was "political," essentially because the text of the Constitution did not answer the question and the subject was foreign affairs.[40]

Nixon v. United States[41] refused to review the Senate's conviction of a federal judge in an impeachment trial.   The majority held that the Constitution's grant to the Senate of "sole power" to try impeachments excluded the courts not

---

[39] 409 U.S. 1 (1972).

[40] Goldwater v. Carter, 444 U.S. 996 (1979).

[41] 506 U.S. 224 (1993).

only from trying impeachments but also from reviewing Senate judgments. The conclusion was no surprise; impeachment had long been a textbook example of a matter committed for final decision to Congress rather than to the courts.

Less convincingly, the Court added that Article I provided no justiciable standards for determining whether the full Senate had to hear evidence in an impeachment case. Justice White seemed quite right in protesting that the purpose of the Sole-Power Clause was to keep impeachment trials out of the courts, not to prescribe how the Senate should take evidence. He wryly observed that if any branch has the expertise to determine what it means to "try" a case, it is the judiciary.

Congress has waded into the battle over whether the United States should recognize Jerusalem as Israel's capital, enacting a law that allowed Jerusalem-born Americans to list Israel as their place of birth. The Secretary of State declined to enforce the statute and, defending an action under the statute, argued that the case presented a political question; the lower courts agreed. The Court unanimously disagreed, finding that judicially manageable standards exist,

allowing the judiciary to act.[42]   Justice So-
tomayor's concurring opinion analyzed all six
Baker factors, criticizing the Court's opinion as
insufficiently demanding for failing to do so.
That case merely decided justiciability; when it
returned to the Court three years later,[43] a badly
split Court ruled that the statute infringed the
President's exclusive power to recognize foreign
governments, handing the plaintiff a loss on
separation-of-powers instead of the political-
question grounds.

Whether there are adequate standards to
permit effective judicial review depends in large
part on one's view of the merits. For example,
there is no lack of standards for reapportionment cases, provided one agrees with the Court
that the Constitution basically mandates nu-
merical equality among districts. It is more difficult to find standards if one thinks, as Justice
Frankfurter did, that the apportionment process
must take account of many complicated demo-
graphic and geographical factors.

There is tension between the political-
question theory and the perception of courts as
guardians of the Constitution. Except where the

---

[42] Zivotofsky *ex rel.* Zivotofsky v. Clinton, 132 S. Ct. 1421
(2012).

[43] Zivotofsky *ex rel.* Zivotofsky v. Kerry, 135 S. Ct. 2076
(2015).

Constitution commits the matter to the discretion of another branch (the first *Baker* criterion), characterizing an issue as political means that the executive or the legislature may violate the Constitution without concern about judicial oversight. *Baker* recognized the argument that judicial review is indispensable to enforcing the Constitution in regard to legislative apportionment, which the Court previously considered "political." But in many malapportioned states, the political processes were not fully open because of the malapportionment. In states lacking machinery to bypass the legislature to amend their constitutions, legislative reapportionment would have consolidated some legislative districts. Some legislators would have been voting to extinguish their own seats.

B. Judicial Review

While holding that there was no jurisdiction to issue an original writ of mandamus to a federal officer, *Marbury v. Madison*[44] concluded that federal courts had the power and the duty to determine federal statutes' constitutionality. Chief Justice Marshall traced this authority to four constitutional sources. (1) Marshall described judicial review as inherent in written constitutions; yet the French constitution,

---

[44] 5 U.S. (1 Cranch) 137 (1803).

adopted just a few years before, expressly forbade the judges to meddle with legislation. He relied also on (2) Article III's provision extending the judicial power to constitutional cases, (3) Article VI's requirement that the judges swear to uphold the Constitution, and (4) the Supremacy Clause, which makes only laws enacted "pursuant to" the Constitution the supreme law of the land.

At the time of the Constitutional Convention, there were precedents for judicial review of municipal, colonial, and state legislation by analogy to the familiar *ultra wires* doctrine in corporate law. The Convention records confirm widespread expectation that the courts would review the constitutionality of federal laws. For example, in arguing against a Council of Revision to review federal statutes, Rufus King of Massachusetts insisted that "the Judges will have the expounding of those laws when they come before them; and they will no doubt stop the operation of such as shall appear repugnant to the Constitution." James Madison said much the same thing in the House of Representatives in proposing the Bill of Rights in 1789.

Judicial review is firmly established, and the legitimacy argument is strong. Yet a crucial ambiguity remains in *Marbury*, relevant to important federal-courts issues.   At one point,

Marshall appeared to treat judicial review as a mere byproduct of the traditional judicial function of deciding cases. Marshall said that to decide a case, a court must determine what the law is; if a statute conflicts with the Constitution, it is not the law, as the latter is supreme.

Elsewhere, however, he treats judicial review as an indispensable element in the constitutional scheme of checks and balances. Express limitations on legislative authority would be worthless if the courts were required to enforce unconstitutional laws: "It would be giving to the legislature a practical and real omnipotence, with the same breath which professes to restrict their powers within narrow limits. It is prescribing limits, and declaring that those limits may be passed at pleasure." Alexander Hamilton had said the same thing in the Federalist: "The courts were designed to be an intermediate body between the people and the legislature, in order * * * to keep the latter within the limits assigned to their authority."

If judicial review is nothing more than a clean-hands doctrine—a requirement that judges not violate the Constitution—then there is no cause for concern if Congress (1) strips the Supreme Court of jurisdiction to decide constitutional cases, (2) packs it with additional Justices of its own persuasion, or—as it did in 1802—

(3) rearranges the Court's terms so that for fourteen months it will not sit at all. If judicial review is an essential part of the Framers' plan to keep other branches from exceeding their powers, however, any such measure poses a grave threat to the Constitution.

III. CONGRESSIONAL CONTROL OF FEDERAL JURISDICTION

The Constitution creates only the Supreme Court, so the Convention delegates generally described the realm of federal judicial functioning in broad categories. Because there were not necessarily going to be any inferior federal courts, the Constitution could not proceed on the assumption that they would exist. Accordingly, Article III, § 2, cl. 1, describes kinds of cases—federal-question, diversity, federal government as a party, etc.—without actually *vesting* jurisdiction in any inferior court. That is why the jurisdiction of any Article III court other than the Supreme Court must rest on a vesting statute, which itself comply with Article III. Thus, it is never correct simply to assert that a district or circuit court has jurisdiction under Article III; there must always be a statute specifically conferring jurisdiction. The Constitution itself vests jurisdiction only in the Supreme Court, and protects only the Court's original jurisdiction from congressional control.

From time to time there are proposals to restrict the Supreme Court's appellate jurisdiction, usually because their proponents disapprove of the way the Court has decided cases in a particular area. In 1964, a congressman introduced a bill to deprive all of the federal courts of jurisdiction to hear reapportionment cases. In the late 1950s, a Senate bill proposed depriving the Supreme Court of jurisdiction over bar admissions, state subversion laws, congressional-committee cases, and cases involving the Federal Loyalty-Security Program. Neither passed.

A. Taking Cases Away from the Federal Courts

The question has always been how much Congress can limit federal jurisdiction. Several old cases upheld congressional restrictions, but the restrictions were limited. *Sheldon v. Sill*[45] upheld the Assignee Clause of the Judiciary Act of 1789, forbidding creating diversity jurisdiction by assigning claims to persons with more "helpful" citizenships.[46] In The Federalist, Hamilton had noted the danger such assignments would pose. *Ex parte McCardle*[47] approved a statute withdrawing some habeas corpus cases from the Supreme Court's review jurisdiction. The Court pointed out, however, that review of such decisions was still possible under other sections of law, and *Ex parte Yerger*[48] upheld the Court's jurisdiction to review such cases under the All Writs Act.

---

[45] 49 U.S. (8 How.) 441 (1850).

[46] *See* 28 U.S.C. § 1359.

[47] 74 U.S. (7 Wall.) 506 (1869).

[48] 75 U.S. (8 Wall.) 85 (1868).

Lockerty v. Phillips[49] upheld Congress's power to give the Emergency Court of Appeals exclusive jurisdiction over suits attacking regulations under a wartime price-control statute, but that was really a venue measure. Congress directed cases that otherwise could have gone to federal district courts or to state trial courts to the ECA. Appeals ran directly to the Supreme Court.

Yakus v. United States[50] is more troubling. The Emergency Price Control Act forbade district courts hearing criminal charges arising under the Act to entertain defenses attacking the price-control regulations as invalid. The Court found no due process violation because the defendants could have protested to the Price Administrator and, if refused relief, could have sued in the ECA. The Court based its decision on the familiar waiver principle that a litigant who fails to take timely advantage of existing remedies may not thereafter seek a second opportunity. The Court also strongly implied that a decision of the ECA in the protestant's favor would have preclusive effect in a subsequent criminal prosecution. Thus, none of these four

---

[49] 319 U.S. 182 (1943).

[50] 321 U.S. 414 (1944).

cases stands for the proposition that Congress has broad power to deny federal jurisdiction.

Dictum in *Martin v. Hunter's Lessee*[51] typifies one argument against such power. Justice Story was attempting to reconcile the clauses of Article III. He acknowledged that neither the lower courts nor the Supreme Court had to have jurisdiction over all matters within the scope of Article III. But the first clause of the Article is mandatory: the judicial power (presumably all of it since there is no modifier) *"shall* be vested. . . ." (Emphasis added.) Thus, Congress could remove jurisdiction of classes of cases either from the Supreme Court or from the inferior federal courts, but not from both. But that has never been the law. For example, the federal courts have lacked jurisdiction over diversity cases where the amount in controversy is insufficient. It is difficult to see why the Framers would have wanted to forbid such a manner of conserving judicial resources.

It seems clear is that Congress cannot deny jurisdiction on any basis that itself would violate an individual constitutional right. For example, Article I, § 9, forbids Congress to suspend the writ of habeas corpus except under very limited conditions. Congress would offend that provi-

---

[51] 14 U.S. (1 Wheat.) 304 (1816).

sion if it closed all federal courts to certain habeas claims. *Battaglia v. General Motors Corp.*[52] appeared to generalize that principle when it upheld the Portal-to-Portal Act. The Supreme Court had given a surprisingly broad reading to the Fair Labor Standards Act, creating a windfall benefit for employees and an unexpected burden for employers. Congress amended the statute to abolish that burden, and it did so retroactively. In an attempt to avoid judicial review of the repealer, Congress purported to remove from all federal and state courts jurisdiction to enforce the original statute.

The court found no due-process violation in the repealer. But, it reached the merits despite Congress's apparent prohibition of jurisdiction, reasoning that Congress's power to limit federal jurisdiction, like all its other powers, failed when it clashed with due process. That argument applies equally to other constitutional provisions. To close the courts to claims of constitutional violation effectively denies the substantive constitutional right. The judicial-guardian theory of *Marbury v. Madison* views judicial review as an essential tool for keeping the majoritarian branches from overrunning constitutional limits.

---

[52] 169 F.2d 254 (2d Cir. 1948).

The Convention clearly expected the federal judiciary to maintain the uniformity and supremacy of federal law, and the Supreme Court was the focus of that expectation. That view suggests that Congress can make only minor procedural adjustments like the jurisdictional-amount requirement. Professor Henry Hart noted that the Exceptions Clause could not destroy "the essential role of the Supreme Court in the constitutional plan."

United States v. Klein[53] lends further support to that idea. A Reconstruction statute permitted recovery of federally-seized property taken during the Civil War upon proof that the owner had not supported the rebellion; the Supreme Court held that a Presidential pardon was satisfactory proof. Congress amended the statute to disallow pardons as proof and purported to deny all courts jurisdiction to return property to someone with a pardon. The Court held the amended statute unconstitutional, because it attempted both to dictate the result in pending cases and to limit the effect of a pardon. Because the statute closed all avenues of relief (unlike in *McCardle*), it denied substantive rights.

---

[53] 80 U.S. (13 Wall.) 128 (1872).

Justice Rutledge's *Yakus* dissent proposed a narrower reading of *Klein*. It distinguished taking away a court's jurisdiction entirely from giving the court jurisdiction but directing it to ignore the Constitution in deciding. The latter would offend even *Marbury*'s narrow judicial-clean-hands aspect: at a minimum, judges must follow the Constitution. One can read *Klein* as applying that principle, because the statute required the Supreme Court to exercise jurisdiction and to dismiss the entire case rather than simply dismissing the appeal.

B. Taking Remedies Away from the Federal Courts

Congress sometimes limits federal courts' jurisdiction by restricting the remedies they may grant. The oldest example is the Anti-Injunction Act, which Congress passed in 1793.[54] The default position is that federal courts should not stay state-court proceedings, subject to three exceptions that the Court interprets very strictly: (1) if Congress expressly authorizes injunctions,[55] (2) "where necessary in aid of its juris-

---

[54] The current version is 28 U.S.C. § 2283.

[55] In one famous case, Mitchum v. Foster, 407 U.S. 225 (1972), the Court fudged, finding in effect that the Civil Rights Act, 42 U.S.C. § 1983, by authorizing a "suit in equity," clearly intended to remove the bar of Anti-Injunction Act. One commentator noted that the Court had recognized an "implied ex-

diction" (which the Court has strictly limited to *rem* cases, where the federal court has attached property and a state court later tries to adjudicate with respect to the same property), and (3) "to protect or effectuate its judgments" (limited to use when a federal judgment is preclusive on a claim or an issue and a state court attempts to relitigate).

In 28 U.S.C. §§ 1341 (the Tax Injunction Act) and 1342 (the Johnson Act), Congress, on grounds of federalism, forbade federal courts to restrain enforcing state taxes and many state public-utility rate orders, when state courts provided a "plain, speedy, and efficient remedy." *Lauf v. E.G. Shinner & Co.*[56] upheld the Norris-LaGuardia Act, which deprived federal courts of jurisdiction to issue injunctions in certain labor disputes. In dictum, the Court mentioned that "there can be no question of the power of Congress thus to define and limit the jurisdiction" of federal courts. *Lauf* is authoritative, however, only for the proposition that the limitation that the Norris-LaGuardia Act imposed was constitutional.

---

press exception—an oxymoron if ever there was one."

[56] 303 U.S. 323 (1938).

IV. SUBJECT-MATTER JURISDICTION

A.   Article III Courts

   1. The Constitutional Scope of Permissible Jurisdiction

Article III, § 2, describes the reach of federal judicial power but, with the exception of the Supreme Court, it does not actually *vest* subject-matter jurisdiction in any court. That is understandable; since the Constitution leaves creation of other federal courts in Congress's hands (Art. III, § 1), it could hardly vest jurisdiction in courts not certain to exist. Article III, § 2, therefore, describes the *potential* jurisdictional reach of inferior federal courts but leaves to Congress the task of making that potential jurisdiction real.

Article III, § 2, refers to "cases" and to "controversies." What is the difference? There is little practical difference, though there is some indication that controversies include only civil actions. Justice Joseph Story noticed that the section speaks of jurisdiction over "all" cases of three types—(1) federal-question, (2) officials of foreign government, and (3) admiralty/maritime cases—but omits "all" when describing six types of "controversies": (1) United States as a party, (2) disputes among states, (3) disputes between a state and a citizen of a different state, (4) diversity cases, (5) where state boundaries were not clear, disputes among co-citizens claiming land under grants from different states, and

(6) alienage jurisdiction. He suggested that Congress was constitutionally obliged to vest "case" jurisdiction in inferior federal courts, though it could omit "controversies" because of "all's" absence. No one listened.

From the beginning, Congress did not vest all of the power that the Constitution would have permitted. For example, the Judiciary Act of 1789 established the inferior federal courts and granted diversity jurisdiction, but the amount in controversy had to exceed $500.[57] The Constitution makes no mention of a jurisdictional floor. Congress subsequently raised the floor in steps, first to $2,000, and then successively to $3,000, $10,000, $50,000 and $75,000, where it stands today.

There was no omnibus grant of federal-question jurisdiction in the 1789 Act, though other individual statutes granted narrow slivers of it—conferring federal-question "retail," if you will. The outgoing Federalist Congress in 1801 did create what we would today recognize as general federal-question jurisdiction; the incoming Jeffersonian Congress promptly repealed the grant in 1802. When Congress did finally create "wholesale" federal-question jurisdiction in 1875, it mandated the same monetary jurisdictional floor as for diversity jurisdiction, and the two moved in lockstep until 1980, when Con-

---

[57] That is roughly $6,900 is 2014 dollars.

gress abolished the amount-in-controversy requirement for federal-question cases.

2. Original Jurisdiction

a. The Supreme Court

Article III, § 2, cl. 2, describes a limited class of cases in which the Supreme Court has original jurisdiction: "Cases affecting Ambassadors, other public Ministers and Consuls, and those in which a State shall be Party * * * ." With respect to the states, despite the apparently unconditional language of the Constitution, the controversy must be within the more general description of the judicial power in Clause 2. Congress has no power either to expand or to curtail the Court's original jurisdiction. All other types of cases that Article III mentions reach the Supreme Court only through the appellate process. Even in cases within the Court's original jurisdiction, there is rarely a typical trial scene within the Court's chamber. Most often, the Court refers the fact-finding process to a special master who reports back to the Court suggesting a disposition. Special masters' reports receive considerable deference from the Court, making the Court's approach in such cases seem more like appellate review than *de novo* consideration.

b. The District Courts

(1) Invoking Federal Jurisdiction

There are two ways litigants can invoke the district court's jurisdiction: originally or by removal from a state court. It is a common mistake to regard removal as some special kind of jurisdiction; it is not. It simply is a method for defendants to invoke federal jurisdiction in most cases that plaintiffs could have filed originally in federal court but chose not to. The general rule is that any case within the original jurisdiction of the district courts is removable if all of the defendants agree to removal.[58] Thus, 28 U.S.C. § 1441 does not *confer* or *vest* jurisdiction in the district court; it creates a procedure by which defendants may invoke the jurisdiction Congress has already conferred on the district court, commonly in 28 U.S.C. §§ 1331–1338.

It is critically important to remember that the federal courts decide subject-matter jurisdiction on a claim-by-claim basis, not on a case-by-case basis. *Every claim* in a district court must have a statutory "ticket of admission." There are *no* exceptions to that rule. Now, the ticket may say § 1331 or § 1332 or any other statute

---

[58] The best known exception to that rule is that a case sounding purely in diversity is not removable if *any* defendant is a citizen of the forum state. Congress has also made some limited categories of cases nonremovable—those involving the Federal Employers' Liability Act, workers' compensation being the most notable.

that vests jurisdiction in the district court; but there must be a ticket for each claim. There is one special kind of ticket: 28 U.S.C. § 1367, the supplemental jurisdiction statute. The airlines refer to this as a "companion ticket," meaning that the claim can come into the district court, but only if it accompanies a claim over which the district court has stand-alone jurisdiction and bears the proper relationship to that claim ("common nucleus of operative fact"). A discussion of supplemental jurisdiction appears at pages 74 and 85.

(2) Federal-Question Jurisdiction

(i) The Well-Pleaded-Complaint Rule

Both Article III and 28 U.S.C. § 1331 mention federal-question cases, and in similar wording. Article III refers to "all Cases, in Law and Equity, arising under this Constitution, the Laws of the United States, and Treaties made, or which shall be made, under their authority * * * ." Section 1331 speaks of "all civil actions arising under the Constitution, laws, or treaties of the United States."[59] Despite the similarity, the Court has never interpreted § 1331 to be as broad as the constitutional language. The legislative history of § 1331 consists only of two sen-

---

[59] Federal question jurisdiction tracked the amount-in-controversy requirement of the diversity jurisdiction statute until 1980, when Congress eliminated the requirement from federal-question cases.

tences, in which the Senate's President *pro tempore* stated that Congress intended the statute to embrace all of the constitutionally permissible territory, but it has not been so.

The critical words in both sections are "arising under," and the phrase's meaning has changed over time. In the nineteenth century, the Court at first only required that a matter of federal law appear in the case, but it soon narrowed its approach to require that the federal matter was a necessary part of the "well-pleaded" complaint. An allegation is well-pleaded if its omission from the complaint would subject the complaint to dismissal for failure to state a claim; that is simply another way of testing whether the allegation is essential to the complaint or is surplusage.[60]

The case best known for that rule is *Louisville & Nashville R. Co. v. Mottley*,[61] in which the plaintiffs predicted that the railroad would defend based on federal law and offered federal law rebuttals to the anticipated defense. The

---

[60] When I teach Civil Procedure and Federal Courts, I use a surgery metaphor. If you were a surgeon, and you wanted to know whether a particular organ was essential to your patient, one way to find out would be to remove it. If the patient then died, you would doubtless say something like, "Oh, my goodness gracious, that organ was essential." As an attorney, the complaint is your patient, and each of its allegations is an organ. The advantage you have over the surgeon is that you can later replace the missing organ, reviving the "patient."

[61] 211 U.S. 149 (1908).

Court ruled that there was no jurisdiction. *Mottley* exemplifies how to test whether allegations are essential to a complaint. The facts of the case were simple. In 1871, the plaintiffs were injured in a railroad accident. They reached a settlement with the railroad under which they would be entitled to transportation for life in exchange for not suing the railroad for negligence. All went well until 1906 when, as a part of President Roosevelt's trust-busting efforts, Congress passed a statute forbidding railroads from giving free transportation.[62] In 1907, the railroad did not send the Mottleys their annual passes. The Mottleys sued.

Step 1 is drafting the complaint. The complaint, boiled down to colloquial language, looked like this:

---

[62] There is also some indication that Congress passed the statute to prevent its members from receiving free transportation and thus becoming beholden to the railroads. That may have been the last time Congress acted seriously to enforce ethical standards with respect to its members.

1. We have a contract with the Railroad.

2. We agreed not to sue the Railroad, and we didn't.

3. The Railroad agreed to give us transportation passes for life.

4. The Railroad now refuses to give us the passes.

5. The Railroad relies on the 1906 statute forbidding free transportation.

6. The statute is prospective only and does not apply to contracts made before its effective date.

7. Even if it does apply, our transportation is not free; we did pay for it within the meaning of the statute by giving up our causes of action for negligence.

8. If the court rejects the allegation in Paragraph 7, then the statute is unconstitutional as a taking without just compensation.

WHEREFORE, give us the passes.

It isn't fancy, but it does reflect the controversy.

Step 2 is to ask whether, if everything the complaint alleges is true and there is nothing additional, the plaintiffs are entitled to relief.[63] Under this complaint, the plaintiffs are entitled to relief.

Step 3 involves striking from the complaint anything having to do with federal law and any other allegations that may be surplusage. In this case, ¶¶ 5-8 concern federal law. Now the complaint looks like this:

---

[63] You will recognize this as today's Federal Rule 12(b)(6) inquiry in colloquial language.

1. We have a contract with the Railroad.

2. We agreed not to sue the Railroad, and we didn't.

3. The Railroad agreed to give us transportation passes for life.

4. The Railroad now refuses to give us the passes.

5. ~~The Railroad relies on the 1906 statute forbidding free transportation.~~

6. ~~The statute is prospective only and does not apply to contracts made before its effective date.~~

7. ~~Even if it does apply, our transportation is not free; we did pay for it within the meaning of the statute by giving up our causes of action for negligence.~~

8. ~~If the court rejects the allegation in Paragraph 7, then the statute is unconstitutional as a taking without just compensation.~~

WHEREFORE, give us the passes.

Step 4 is to ask the Step-2 question again. If everything that the modified complaint alleges is true *and there is nothing additional*,[64] are the

---

[64] This is the hard part, because one knows that that there are additional issues in the case. Remember, though, that the

plaintiffs entitled to relief? On the remaining allegations, the answer is pretty clearly that the plaintiffs are still entitled to relief; the modified complaint states everything necessary for a claim sounding in contract. Well, what does that mean? All those allegations about federal law, which certainly will have a major effect on the outcome of the dispute, are nonetheless not necessary to enable the plaintiffs to state a claim; the underlying claim is a simple contract claim. The federal allegations are not "well-pleaded," and the case does not qualify for jurisdiction under 28 U.S.C. § 1331.

Caveat: This method works for all complaints seeking coercive relief (i.e. relief compelling the defendant to do something, whether it is paying a money judgment, refraining from taking action injurious to the plaintiff's interests (a negative injunction), or compelling performance of a certain action (a mandatory injunction). This method will not work directly for a complaint seeking declaratory relief. The procedure there has two additional steps. See infra page 61, subsection (5).

---

object of this exercise is to see whether the plaintiffs can "state a claim upon which relief may be granted" without reference to federal law or other matter that may come up as a defense, not to try the case.

(ii) A Brief Detour

Eight years after *Mottley*, the Court considered whether a cause of action created by state law could nonetheless qualify as a federal-question case.[65] The action was essentially for trade libel, but the success or failure of the action ultimately turned on questions of patent law. Justice Holmes' majority opinion stated, "A complaint arises under the law that creates the cause of action." Defamation, of which trade libel is one species, is a state-law claim, so the Court found no jurisdiction. The *American-Well-Works* test is useful as a test of inclusion but not nearly as helpful for purposes of exclusion. That is, if federal law creates the cause of action upon which the plaintiff sues, one can be pretty sure that there is federal-question jurisdiction.[66] But, federal-question jurisdiction may exist even if federal law does not create the cause of action if a federal allegation is nonetheless essential to a state-law claim.

(iii)   The Outcome-Determinative Articulation

Five years after *American Well Works*, the Court considered a derivative action brought by

---

[65] American Well Works Co. v. Layne & Bowler Co., 241 U.S. 257 (1916).

[66] There is a narrow exception in cases in which the federal law is so far in the background of the case as to play no part in the resolution of the dispute.

a Missouri shareholder to prevent the corporate fiduciaries from investing in federal farm loan bonds.[67] With Justice Holmes in anguished dissent, the *Smith* Court found jurisdiction, because the plaintiff was unable to state a claim for relief without alleging the unconstitutionality of bonds. The majority stated that when the plaintiff's well-pleaded complaint rises or falls on a disputed question of federal law, federal-question jurisdiction exists. This outcome-determinative articulation added nothing to the well-pleaded-complaint rule; if the federal matter is well-pleaded, so that eliminating it from the complaint causes the complaint to succumb to a motion to dismiss under Rule 12(b)(6), then obviously if the plaintiff does not prevail on the federal matter, she will lose. Cases in this pattern—a state-created claim with an essential component depending on federal law—are "hybrid" cases.

In 1936, Justice Brandeis summarized the Court's approach to federal-question jurisdiction:

> To bring a case within the statute, a right or immunity created by the Constitution or laws of the United States must be an element, and an essential one, of the plaintiff's cause of action.

---

[67] Smith v. Kansas City Title & Trust Co., 255 U.S. 180 (1921).

The right or immunity must be such that it will be supported if the Constitution or laws of the United States are given one construction or effect, and defeated if they receive another. A genuine and present controversy, not merely a possible or conjectural one, must exist with reference thereto, and the controversy must be disclosed upon the face of the complaint, unaided by the answer or by the petition for removal. Indeed, the complaint itself will not avail as a basis of jurisdiction in so far as it goes beyond a statement of the plaintiff's cause of action and anticipates or replies to a probable defense.[68]

The well-pleaded-complaint rule makes three appearances in that short summary, which also refers to the outcome-determinative test and the necessity that the federal matter be in contested. There, except for declaratory judgment cases, the matter rested for fifty years.

(iv)   Substantiality

Merrell   Dow   Pharmaceuticals,   Inc.   v. Thompson[69] was another hybrid case. The

---

[68] Gully v. First Nat'l Bank, 299 U.S. 109, 112-13 (1936) (citations omitted).

[69] 478 U.S. 804 (1986).

plaintiffs were families with children allegedly damaged *in utero* because their mothers took Bendectin. The plaintiffs asserted claims for negligence *per se* on the ground that the defendant had mislabeled the drug, in violation of the Food, Drug and Cosmetic Act (FDCA). The allegation of mislabeling was necessary to that count of the complaint, outcome-determinative, and in contest between the parties. Justice Brandeis's spirit smiled. And yet, the Court ruled against federal-question jurisdiction because the mislabeling issue was not sufficiently "substantial." Before *Merrell Dow*, "substantiality" for federal-question cases meant only what Justice Brandeis had said—that the issue was well-pleaded, outcome-determinative and in contest. The *Merrell-Dow* majority concluded that since FDCA provided no private right of action, Congress intended no federal-question jurisdiction in hybrid cases based on the statute.[70] No one seemed sure what "substantiality" was; the only clear thing was that *Merrell Dow* did not have it. That left the jurisdictional status of hybrid cases in considerable doubt.

---

[70] Whether that assumption was correct or not, the Court's reasoning was faulty. The 1938 Congress passed FDCA, and it gave no indication that it was thinking about federal-question jurisdiction at the time. Section 1331 came from Congress in 1875. Why the unexpressed-but-assumed intent of the 1938 Congress is relevant to construing an 1875 statute remains a mystery.

Some lower courts inferred that the Supreme Court had returned to Justice Holmes's law-that-creates-the-cause-of-action test. The Court returned to the hybrid-case problem, although it took almost two decades to do so. *Grable & Sons Metal Products, Inc. v. Darue Engineering & Manufacturing*[71] was a quiet title action—a property claim clearly sounding in state law. The defendant had acquired the property at a tax delinquency sale, but the plaintiff claimed that the sale was invalid because the plaintiff did not receive notice in the manner 26 U.S.C. § 6335 required.[72] The federal question was whether certified mail service satisfied the statute.

As in *Merrell Dow*, the statute provided no private right of action, so the Court might have ruled against jurisdiction. It did not.[73] A unanimous Court[74] found that the federal question was substantial, although it warned that even that might not suffice to establish jurisdiction unless asserting federal jurisdiction was "con-

---

[71] 545 U.S. 308 (2005).

[72] The plaintiff did get actual notice, but only by certified mail, whereas the statute appeared to require either personal service or by leaving the notice at the owner's home or business.

[73] Justice Souter's opinion declared that *Merrell Dow* was not a *sub silentio* return to the Holmes test.

[74] Justice Thomas concurred but also said he favored returning to the Holmes test because it is clear. He did not discuss how successful that test might be in including cases that federal courts should hear and excluding those they should not.

sistent with congressional judgment about the sound division of labor between state and federal courts governing the application of § 1331."[75] What made the federal issue substantial? The Court noted several factors. First, prompt, certain collection of federal taxes is vital to the government. Second, the government has "a direct interest in the availability of a federal forum"— both a home-court-advantage interest and an interest in having federal judges' expertise on federal tax law questions. Third, "since it will be the rare state title case that raises a contested matter of federal law, federal jurisdiction * * * will portend only a microscopic effect on the federal-state division of labor." That is somewhat counter-intuitive; one might expect that the more often a question of federal law will come up, the more important it is to have federal expertise, but because the Court focused on workload effect, its conclusion is at least understandable.

Grable appeared to open up jurisdictional possibilities many thought lost after *Merrell*

---

[75] Once again, as in Note 70, one confronts the anachronism problem. The opinion does not suggest that the Congress that passed the Internal Revenue Code in 1954 or any of the Congresses that have amended it since were thinking about division-of-labor problems when they considered § 6335. The 1875 Congress, from which today's § 1331 comes, was thinking about the jurisdictional implications of tax litigation, since there was no income tax in 1875, and it took the Sixteenth Amendment (1913) to authorize one.

Dow. Enterprising counsel sought to take advantage of that liberalization, so in 2013, the Court returned to the topic. *Gunn v. Minton*[76] asked "whether a state law claim alleging legal malpractice in the handling of a patent claim must be brought in federal court." A unanimous Court found no federal jurisdiction. Chief Justice Roberts wrote for the Court, making what be the most intelligent statement by a Justice on federal-question jurisdiction since 1936. He addressed himself to hybrid cases: "In outlining the contours of this slim category, we do not paint on a blank canvas. Unfortunately, the canvas looks like one that Jackson Pollock got to first."[77] The Chief Justice offered a four-part consideration of whether federal-question exists in a hybrid case, drawing on *Grable*. "[F]ederal jurisdiction over a state law claim will lie if a federal issue is: (1) necessarily raised, (2) actually disputed,   (3) substantial,   and (4) capable of resolution in federal court without disrupting the federal-state balance approved by Congress." That is the good news.

The bad news is that the "test" does not help counsel or judges make the critical judgment.

---

76 133 S. Ct. 1059 (2013).

77 Jackson Pollock was an American abstract artist in the mid-twentieth century. He was famous for his style of "drip painting." (Others characterized his paintings as "splatter.") If you find the Court's treatment of hybrid cases confusing, this should reassure you that your perception is 100% accurate.

The first two parts come from the *Mottley-Smith-Gully* line; they are unremarkable. The last two parts are sufficiently amorphous to render them unpredictable. Thus, it is still possible for an outcome-determinative federal issue that the parties contest to appear in a well-pleaded complaint in a hybrid action without there being federal-question jurisdiction.

(v) Declaratory-Judgment Cases

(A) Under the Federal Declaratory Judgment Act

Federal-question jurisdiction in declaratory-judgment cases has all of the complexity seen in coercive actions like *Mottley*, *American Well Works*, *Smith*, *Gully*, *Merrell Dow*, *Grable*, and *Gunn*, with one extra twist. *Skelly Oil Co. v. Phillips Petroleum Co.*[78] held that Congress did not intend the federal Declaratory Judgment Act to expand federal jurisdiction.[79] The Court meant that no cases should qualify for federal-question jurisdiction under the Act that could not have qualified without it—in other words, if they were coercive actions. At first blush, that may not seem very significant, but pleadings in declaratory-judgment cases are different. *Skelly* provides an example. Stripped to its essentials,

---

[78] 339 U.S. 667 (1950).

[79] The extensive legislative history of the Declaratory Judgment Act demonstrates that the Court's conclusion is wrong, *but it is the law.*

the case involved a contract under which Phillips was to purchase natural gas from Skelly to sell to a local pipe line company that wanted to construct a new pipe line and needed a certificate of "public convenience and necessity" from the Federal Power Commission to do so. The contract between Phillips and Skelly provided that Skelly had a right to cancel the contract after a fixed date if the FPC had not yet issued the certificate. One day before that date, the FPC announced, "A certificate of public convenience and necessity be and it is hereby issued to applicant upon the terms and conditions of this order * * * ," but there was a catch. The FPC made the announcement, it did not release the content of the order for two more days. In the interim, Skelly had notified Phillips that it was canceling the contract. Phillips commenced a federal declaratory-judgment action to declare that the contract still in effect.

Using the technique outlined on page 49 helps demonstrate the problem. Here is the essence of the Phillips complaint (Step 1):

> 1. Phillips has a contract with Skelly.
>
> 2. Skelly agreed to supply Phillips with natural gas.
>
> 3. Phillips agreed to pay Skelly a stated rate for the natural gas.
>
> 4. Skelly has an option to cancel the contract on or after December 1.
>
> 5. Skelly's option to cancel expires if FPC issues a certificate before Skelly exercises the option.
>
> 6. The FPC issued the certificate on November 30.
>
> 7. Skelly purported to cancel on December 2.
>
> WHEREFORE, declare the contract still in effect.

Step 2: If everything the complaint alleges is true and there is nothing additional, is the plaintiff entitled to relief? It should be clear that the answer is "yes"; Skelly attempted to exercise its option *after* the FPC issued the certificate. So, Phillips does state a claim upon which relief may be granted.

Step 3: Strike out all the federal matter.

> 1. Phillips has a contract with Skelly.
> 2. Skelly agreed to supply Phillips with natural gas.
> 3. Phillips agreed to pay Skelly a stated rate for the natural gas.
> 4. Skelly has an option to cancel the contract on or after December 1.
> 5. Skelly's option to cancel expires if FPC issues a certificate before Skelly exercises the option.
> ~~6. The FPC issued the certificate on November 30.~~
> 7. Skelly purported to cancel on December 2.
> WHEREFORE, declare the contract still in effect.

Paragraph 6 is the only federal allegation. The single issue in the case was whether the date of the announcement (November 30), the date the contents of the order become public (December 2), or the date by which the certificate grantee accepts or satisfies the conditions (some later time) was the effective certificate date.

Step 4: With the federal matter stricken, does the modified complaint still state a claim upon which relief may be granted? It does not. A judge, upon hearing the remaining six allegations and being asked to declare the contract still in effect might well respond, "Why should I? Skelly canceled." Note the difference between

Skelly and *Mottley* on this point. Removing the federal matter from the *Mottley* complaint still left the plaintiffs with a perfectly valid contact action. Removing the federal matter from the *Skelly* complaint causes it no longer to state a claim for relief.

Thus, the federal allegation in the *Skelly* declaratory-judgment complaint *is* well-pleaded, outcome-determinative, and contested. So before substantiality in its present (formless) form became a factor in 1986, the declaratory-judgment complaint (with Paragraph 6) did appear to qualify for federal-question jurisdiction under § 1331. But wait! The analysis is not quite finished. Declaratory judgment actions often require allegations in the complaint that would be surplusage in the corresponding coercive actions. Is this dispute an example of that?

Because *Skelly* ruled that no declaratory-judgment cases should qualify under § 1331 unless the corresponding coercive case was federal, it is necessary to consider how the complaint would have looked had there been no Declaratory Judgment Act. The action might have arisen in two ways. Upon Skelly's notice of cancellation, Phillips might have commenced an action seeking specific performance based on the anticipatory breach. Alternatively, Phillips might have waited until Skelly actually did not perform, purchased natural gas from some other supplier, and brought a contract action against

Skelly for the amount Phillips had to pay over the original contract price.[80] It does not matter which tactical avenue Phillips would have followed; the complaints would be virtually identical except for the type of relief sought. So let us assume that Phillips waited until the natural gas was due from Skelly and then sued. Step 1: draft the hypothetical complaint.

---

[80] Skelly tried to cancel precisely because the market price of natural gas had risen since the parties contracted.

1. Phillips has a contract with Skelly.

2. Skelly agreed to supply Phillips with natural gas.

3. Phillips agreed to pay Skelly a stated rate for the natural gas.

4. Skelly has an option to cancel the contract on or after December 1.

5. Skelly's option to cancel expires if FPC issues a certificate before Skelly exercises the option.

6. The FPC issued the certificate on November 30.

7. Skelly purported to cancel on December 2.

8. Skelly failed and refused to supply the natural gas when its performance was due.

9. Phillips had to acquire the natural gas from another supplier at a price exceeding the contract price with Skelly.

WHEREFORE, Phillips is entitled to damages in the amount of the difference between the contract price and the price that Phillips had to pay when Skelly breached.

Step 2: If everything the complaint alleges is true and there is nothing additional, is the plaintiff entitled to relief? It should be clear that the answer is "yes"; the complaint recites that Skelly attempted to exercise its option *after* the FPC issued the certificate. So, the coercive action does state a claim upon which relief may be granted.

Step 3: Strike out all the federal matter.

---

1. Phillips has a contract with Skelly.

2. Skelly agreed to supply Phillips with natural gas.

3. Phillips agreed to pay Skelly a stated rate for the natural gas.

4. Skelly has an option to cancel the contract on or after December 1.

5. Skelly's option to cancel expires if FPC issues a certificate before Skelly exercises the option.

~~6. The FPC issued the certificate on November 30.~~

7. Skelly purported to cancel on December 2.

8. Skelly failed and refused to supply the natural gas when Skelly should have performed.

9. Phillips had to acquire the natural gas from another supplier at a price exceeding the contract price with Skelly.

WHEREFORE, Phillips is entitled to damages in the amount of the difference between the contract price and the price that Phillips had to pay when Skelly breached.

Paragraph 6 was still the only federal allegation. The single issue between the parties remains the federal-law question of the effective date of issue.

But because this action began as an action seeking declaratory relief, we need to extend Step 3 to ask whether the hypothetical coercive complaint has any other surplusage. Suppose Phillips pleaded only paragraphs 1-3, 8, and 9. Now the complaint would look like this:

> 1. Phillips has a contract with Skelly.
>
> 2. Skelly agreed to supply Phillips with natural gas.
>
> 3. Phillips agreed to pay Skelly a stated rate for the natural gas.
>
> 4. ~~Skelly has an option to cancel the contract on or after December 1.~~
>
> 5. ~~Skelly's option to cancel expires if FPC issues a certificate before Skelly exercises the option.~~
>
> 6. ~~The FPC issued the certificate on November 30.~~
>
> 7. ~~Skelly purported to cancel on December 2.~~
>
> 8. Skelly failed and refused to supply the natural gas when Skelly should have performed.
>
> 9. Phillips had to acquire the natural gas from another supplier at a price exceeding the contract price with Skelly.
>
> WHEREFORE, Phillips is entitled to damages in the amount of the difference between the contract price and the price that Phillips had to pay when Skelly breached.

Step 4: Does the modified complaint still state a claim upon which relief may be granted? It certainly does. That means that, in addition to the federal allegation of paragraph 6, the allegations of paragraphs 4, 5, and 7 are surplusage. The plaintiff need not make those allegations in order to state a claim. Thus, if Phillips had brought a coercive action rather than a declaratory-judgment action, there would have been no federal-question jurisdiction, because Phillips could state its claim for relief without reference to anything federal.

Does that mean that the stricken paragraphs are irrelevant? Not at all, but ask yourself how that part of the controversy would enter the case. Skelly's lawyers might admit all of the allegations of paragraphs 1-3, 8, and 9, but they certainly would include an affirmative defense in the answer—"there is no contract upon which Phillips can sue; Skelly canceled it." Phillips would then "reply"[81] that the cancellation provision was inoperative because the FPC issued the certificate before the purported cancellation. But note: the federal matter properly enters the case not as part of the complaint or even as part of the answer. Phillips attempts to use the federal matter to defeat an affirmative defense. That is precisely what *Mottley* condemned.

Skelly concluded there was no federal-question jurisdiction in the declaratory-judgment action; to rule otherwise would have allowed federal-question jurisdiction only because of the Declaratory Judgment Act. That

---

[81] FED. R. CIV. P. 7 allows no reply in this circumstance.

conclusion was entirely logical given the Court's (flawed) premise that Congress did not intend the Declaratory Judgment Act to expand federal jurisdiction by embracing cases that would not have qualified for federal-question jurisdiction but for the Declaratory Judgment Act.

The Court's approach means that one must analyze declaratory-judgment cases by drafting an entirely hypothetical coercive complaint, being careful to eliminate from it allegations that—though not surplusage in the declaratory-judgment complaint—are surplusage in the coercive complaint. That is not difficult to do; one simply must remember to do it.

(B) Under State Declaratory Judgment Acts

An ERISA trust had a dispute with a state tax board over whether the trust funds were exempt from a state tax levy.[82] The board filed a two-count complaint in state court. Count 1 requested damages for the levy the trust had ignored; Count 2 requested a declaration under the *state* declaratory judgment act that ERISA does not preempt such levies. The trust removed to the district court on the theory that ERISA preemption was the only issue. When the case reached the Supreme Court, the Justic-

---

[82] Franchise Tax Bd. v. Constr. Laborers Vacation Trust, 463 U.S. 1 (1983).

es had a problem. *Skelly* did not apply by its terms because it rested only on Congress's supposed intent in passing Declaratory Judgment Act. That rationale had no force with respect to a state declaratory judgment act, which the state legislature might well have intended to expand jurisdiction.[83]

So the unanimous Court took the easy way out. Instead of considering what the state legislature intended or the jurisdictional effect that its declaratory-judgment statute had at the state level, the Court decided to use the *Skelly* method for state declaratory-judgment cases. Why? It was "fidelity to its spirit."[84] The Court explained that without the *Skelly* approach, cases that would not qualify for federal jurisdiction under *Skelly* would qualify by relying instead on the comparable state statute.

As a practical matter, this adds one more hypothetical step to analyzing such cases. First,

---

[83] Before leaping to the intuitive (but incorrect) conclusion that states cannot expand federal court jurisdiction in the *Skelly* sense, consider that there are actually two ways in which states do exactly that. First, whenever a state recognizes, through its legislature or as common law, a new cause of action (such as an expanded right to recover for invasion of privacy) it causes more actions to be eligible for federal adjudication as diversity cases. Second, when a state incorporates federal law as an element of a state-created cause of action—a hybrid case—it expands federal-question jurisdiction, subject (of course) to the amorphous substantiality inquiry.

[84] It is not clear whether the Justices actually joined hands around the conference table to summon *Skelly*'s spirit.

one pretends that the state declaratory-judgment case actually sounds under the Declaratory Judgment Act. Then one imagines the corresponding coercive complaint (this is where the colloquial drafting exercise comes in) and analyzes that non-existent complaint using the Court's current method as *Mottley, Smith, Gully, Merrell Dow, Grable,* and *Gunn* have developed it. Good luck.

(3) Supplemental Jurisdiction[85] in Federal-Question Cases

Some cases assert multiple claims. If some of those claims, standing alone, would qualify for subject-matter jurisdiction but others would not, supplemental jurisdiction comes into play. *United Mine Workers v. Gibbs*[86] explained that because Article III refers to "cases" (not claims) arising under federal law, and 28 U.S.C. § 1331 confers jurisdiction over "civil actions," the federal court can adjudicate all of the claims. Thus, as long as multiple claims shared a "common nucleus of operative fact" such that they constituted but one constitutional "case," if even one

---

[85] Originally, the courts talked about "pendent" and "ancillary" jurisdiction. "Pendent jurisdiction" referred to additional claims by the plaintiff against the defendant. "Ancillary jurisdiction" referred to all other possible claim patterns: counterclaims, crossclaims, and claims against and by parties impleaded or otherwise joined after the commencement of the action. The tests for pendent and ancillary jurisdiction were functionally identical.

[86] 383 U.S. 715 (1966).

claim qualified as a stand-alone federal-question claim, the court could hear all of the claims. This avoided the inefficiency of litigating some claims from a single incident in state court and others in federal court. To the extent that the evidence supporting (or refuting) such claims overlaps, having multiple proceedings is inefficient, and the Court has not been willing to force federal-question claims into state courts merely because state claims accompany them.

The genesis of supplemental jurisdiction lies much further back, in *Osborn v. Bank of the United States*.[87] That Court ruled that the mere presence of state-law elements in a claim with federal-law elements did not prevent federal jurisdiction. *Osborn* emphasized that the state and federal elements were parts of a single claim; *Gibbs* broadened that aspect of *Osborn*.

Gibbs allowed some discretion in deciding whether to entertain the state claims, considering (1) whether it would promote convenience and fairness to the litigants, (2) whether the court dismissed the federal claims before trial, (3) whether the state law claims predominated over the federal claims, and (4) the extent to which trying the claims together might produce jury confusion.

---

[87] 22 U.S. (9 Wheat.) 738 (1824).

Almost a quarter of a century after *Gibbs*, Congress codified supplemental jurisdiction in 28 U.S.C. § 1367, which largely echoes the *Gibbs* same-case-or-controversy test as the constitutional justification. But Congress went further, specifically providing that "supplemental jurisdiction shall include claims that involve the joinder or intervention of additional parties," overruling a Court decision that had disallowed the practice. In addition, Congress restricted the district courts' discretion to dismiss a supplemental claim more than *Gibbs* had, limiting discretion to situations where

> (1) the claim raises a novel or complex issue of State law,
>
> (2) the claim substantially predominates over the claim or claims over which the district court has original jurisdiction,
>
> (3) the district court has dismissed all claims over which it has original jurisdiction, or
>
> (4) in exceptional circumstances, there are other compelling reasons for declining jurisdiction.

Although the Supreme Court has not spoken about the fourth criterion, the Ninth Circuit has read it quite narrowly, focusing on Congress's specification of "exceptional circumstances" and "*other* compelling reasons" (emphasis added) as indicating that the default rule is to exercise supplemental jurisdiction and that dismissals under 28 U.S.C. § 1367(c)(4) must be for reasons of import comparable to the enumerated reasons.[88]

(4) Diversity Jurisdiction

Article III, § 2 contemplates diversity jurisdiction; Congress lost no time vesting it in the very first Judiciary Act. The current statute is 28 U.S.C. § 1332. There are two basic requirements: citizenship and amount in controversy. There are four citizenship patterns for plaintiffs and defendants that qualify for diversity jurisdiction: (1) all the plaintiffs are citizens of different states[89] from all defendants,[90] (2) citizens of a state and aliens, generally speaking, (3) citizens of different states with aliens as additional parties, and (4) a foreign state plaintiff and citizens of one or more states as defendants.

---

[88] Executive Software of N. Am., Inc. v. United States District Court for the Central District of California, 24 F.3d 1545 (9th Cir. 1994), *overruled on other grounds*, California Dep't of Water Res. v. Powerex, Inc., 533 F.3d 1087 (9th Cir. 2008).

[89] This is different from "not citizens of the same state." United States citizens domiciled abroad have no state citizenship and cannot be parties in diversity cases.

[90] This is known as the complete-diversity rule, an interpretation of the diversity statute (not Article III) that the Court announced in 1806. If any plaintiff has the same state citizenship as any defendant, the case does not qualify for diversity jurisdiction under § 1332.

(i) Citizenship

(A) Individuals

One must consider three categories of individuals with respect to the citizenship requirement: (1) citizens of the United States, (2) aliens admitted to the United States for permanent residence, and (3) aliens not admitted to the United States for permanent residence.

Citizens of the United States are citizens of a state for diversity purposes if domiciled there. Domicile is the place where one began living with the intention to remain indefinitely—the place one identifies as "home." Individuals may have numerous residences but only one domicile at a time. Domicile remains fixed at one place until the individual acquires a new one, and that is true even if the individual has not lived there for an extended amount of time and even if the individual intends never to return there.[91] The only way to shed an old domicile is to acquire a new one.

Aliens fall into two categories for diversity purposes. Ordinarily, an alien is a citizen or subject of the country of her citizenship. However, if the United States has admitted the alien

---

[91] A person's initial domicile is that of the parents—the domicile of birth—and ordinarily changes with the parents' domicile. At the point when the individual establishes an indefinite residence of the individual's own, that place becomes the individual's domicile.

for permanent residence, then for diversity purposes he is a citizen of the state of his domicile.

(B) Corporations

Corporations may have two state citizenships for diversity purposes. All corporations are citizens of the government that granted their charter. That establishes their place of incorporation. In addition, a corporation is a citizen of the place where the corporate headquarters—the corporation's "home office" or "nerve center"—also known as its principal place of business—are.

(C) Derivative Suits

Shareholders' derivative actions have posed difficult problems under § 1332. In a derivative suit, a shareholder complains that his corporation has failed to sue one or more third parties (usually corporate fiduciaries) who allegedly have damaged it. The shareholder is a plaintiff; the third parties are defendants. The problem is the proper alignment of the corporation.

Nominally the corporation is a defendant. Only corporate fiduciaries can authorize the corporation to become a plaintiff, and since they are almost invariably the defendants from whom damages (payable to the corporation) will come, they are reluctant to authorize the corporate entity to sue them. In that purely formal sense, the corporation's interest opposes the plaintiff's, so the corporation's refusal to sue the third party is a prerequisite to shareholder litigation. On the other hand, the plaintiff seeks no relief from the corporation, and the corporation is the beneficiary of a plaintiff's judgment.

In early cases, the Supreme Court said the corporation should be treated as a plaintiff unless it was "disabled from protecting itself" in that "the very individuals who have a stranglehold over the corporation are the people against whom suit is sought to be brought." *Smith v. Sperling*[92] abandoned this test, complaining that it made jurisdiction turn on the merits. Rather, the corporation is a proper defendant whenever it is "definitely and distinctly opposed to the institution of * * * litigation."[93] Because the shareholder cannot sue unless the corporation refuses to do so, this may mean always. As the dissenters observed, this rule facilitates manufacturing diversity cases, since most corporations have some shareholder who is diverse both to them and to the fiduciaries.

Perhaps the question should be whether the presence of a corporation from the same state as the shareholder or the fiduciary-defendants is likely to affect the sympathies of the triers of fact. Perhaps the corporation's argument is relevant. If a local corporation tells the jury that other defendants are right, a jury may be more

---

[92] 354 U.S. 91 (1957).

[93] Swanson v. Traer, 354 U.S. 114, 116 (1957). *Swanson* was a companion case to *Smith v. Sperling*.

likely to consider their case favorably. But to make alignment depend upon the position the corporation takes at trial would mean the court could determine jurisdiction only after lengthy proceedings, a significant waste of resources. An alternative might be to ignore the corporation (as statutory interpleader ignores the stakeholder's citizenship) and to treat the case as if it were only between the shareholder plaintiffs and the fiduciaries. Such an approach, however, depends upon the assumption that the citizenship of the corporation is unlikely to affect the trier of fact.

(D) Representatives

Estate fiduciaries, guardians *ad litem*, and the like have the citizenship of the party represented.

(ii) Amount in Controversy

The Constitution says nothing about amounts in controversy, but Congress has always insisted that the amount in controversy exceed a certain floor. The original figure was $500, but Congress periodically reenacted the diversity statute with increased amounts, first $2,000, then $3,000, $10,000, $50,000 and finally the present requirement of $75,000. Do not forget that the dispute must *exceed* the floor amount, so that a $75,000 controversy does not qualify for diversity jurisdiction whereas an extra penny makes all the difference.

(A) Test

In cases seeking monetary relief, unless the court concludes to a legal certainty that the plaintiff's case does not exceed the jurisdictional floor, the plaintiff's allegation of a sufficient amount in controversy suffices. Even if the plaintiff ultimately recovers less, the court's jurisdiction does not fail. That is not to say that plaintiffs can simply put large numbers at the ends of their complaints without penalty. If the plaintiff ultimately recovers less than the jurisdictional amount, the court may deny the costs ordinarily taxable against the losing party or even to award costs to the losing party. Those penalties are not automatic; judges tend to impose them only when the plaintiff appears to have alleged the amount in controversy in bad faith.

Cases seeking injunctive or declaratory relief present greater problems. Sometimes the Court looks to the amount it would cost to end the dispute, as in *Healy v. Ratta*,[94] where the Court held that the amount in controversy was the tax that the plaintiff had sued to enjoin rather than either the value of plaintiff's business or of the penalties the plaintiff might incur for refusing to pay the tax. *Healy* declined to consider the value of the tax over a period of years because it would not speculate either that the plaintiff

---

[94] 292 U.S. 263 (1934).

would still be in business or that the state would levy the same tax. On the other hand, in a workers' compensation action on behalf of the victim's widow, the Court did consider future installments even though the widow might die or remarry.

Additional difficulties arise in injunction cases in which one party has a greater stake than the other. When defendant's telegraph wires interfered with plaintiff's property, the Court ruled that even though the cost of removing the wires did not satisfy the amount-in-controversy requirement, the plaintiff's allegation of injury did. Where the plaintiff's economic interest is less than the defendant's, the Court has implied that the defendant's greater amount applies. There is no definitive answer on how to evaluate the jurisdictional amount in "unbalanced" cases.

(B) Aggregation of Claims

A single plaintiff suing a single defendant can aggregate claims to satisfy the jurisdictional amount, even if the claims have no relationship to each other and no claim standing alone exceeds the jurisdictional floor. When the claims arise from the same transaction or occurrence, the rule makes some sense; it is harder to justify when the claims are unrelated. The most one can say in support of the rule then is that applying it is simple and straightforward.

When there are multiple parties on one or both sides, the calculus is more challenging. The Supreme Court permits aggregation only when the parties have a "common undivided interest" or a "single title or right." Note, therefore, that multiple tort victims from the same event cannot aggregate their claims because the claims are several, not joint. By contrast, multiple parties to the same contract may look like they are aggregating, but they really are not. Suppose a contract between five obligees and four obligors, where the total amount of the contract is $100,000. One might intuitively think that each obligee's claim is worth only $20,000, but that is not so. There is a single claim for $100,000 that the obligees hold jointly, so there is no need to "aggregate"; in fact, there is nothing *to* aggregate.

Where does that leave class actions? The Court initially ruled that public utility customers suing for refunds because of a common action of the utility could not aggregate their claims, notwithstanding Rule 23's elimination of the distinctions between true and spurious class actions. *Zahn v. International Paper Co.*[95] went considerably further, holding that even when all of the *named* members of the class independently satisfied the jurisdictional amount, that fact

---

[95] 414 U.S. 291 (1973).

availed the unnamed class members with smaller claims nothing.

ExxonMobil Corp. v. Allapattah Services, Inc.[96] has now held, however (four Justices dissenting), that § 1367, the supplemental jurisdiction statute, overruled *Zahn*, allowing the federal courts to hear diversity class actions as long as at least one named plaintiff satisfies the amount-in-controversy requirement. The Court carefully noted that it based its decision only on §§ 1332 and 1367, not on the Class Action Fairness Act.

(5) Supplemental Jurisdiction in Diversity cases

Congress agreed with the *Zahn* dissenters when it passed the supplemental jurisdiction statute. Supplemental jurisdiction in diversity cases operates differently from federal-question cases. Suppose a three-car accident involving D_1 from State A and D_2 and D_3 from State B.[97] If D_1 sues the other two drivers for negligence, can D_2 assert a negligence crossclaim against D_3? She can. Can D_3 assert a counterclaim against D_1 even if the amount in controversy does not exceed $75,000? He can.

---

[96] 545 U.S. 546 (2005).

[97] For this set of hypotheticals, assume that the plaintiff's claim satisfies the amount-in-controversy requirement.

The only limitation on supplemental jurisdiction in diversity cases comes when the plaintiff asserts a supplemental claim. Suppose that D_2 sues D_1 first. D_2 cannot join D_3 as a defendant; that would destroy complete diversity. But what if D_1 impleads D_3? Now can D_2 file a Rule 14 claim against D_3? Rule 14 allows filing such a claim, but remember that the Federal Rules of Civil Procedure never determine whether there is subject-matter jurisdiction. D_2 cannot file such a claim; where the only ground for subject-matter jurisdiction is diversity, § 1367 excludes claims *by plaintiffs* against parties joined under Rules 14, 19, 20, and 24. A moment's reflection will tell you why. If the statute were otherwise, supplemental jurisdiction would provide an excellent way around the complete-diversity requirement of § 1332. It requires no great leap of imagination to anticipate that D_1 will implead D_3. Congress declined to allow plaintiffs in diversity cases to accomplish indirectly what they could not do directly.

(6) Exclusive Jurisdiction

(i) Generally

In most cases, federal jurisdiction is not exclusive; state courts have concurrent authority. Federal jurisdiction is exclusive, however, in criminal, antitrust, bankruptcy, patent, and copyright cases, as well as in suits against the United States, and in a limited number of admiralty matters. *The Moses Taylor*[98] upheld Congress's power to make federal jurisdiction exclusive, based on Article III and the Necessary and Proper Clause.

The Supreme Court has drawn some rather fine distinctions in administering § 1338(a)'s provision for exclusive federal jurisdiction of cases arising under the patent laws. An action for patent infringement arises under those laws, since the statute both forbids infringement and provides a remedy; federal jurisdiction is exclusive. The same conduct, however, may constitute breach of a patent license, a contract claim, which a federal court cannot hear at all unless the parties satisfy the diversity-jurisdiction requirements.

Moreover, although patent validity is precisely the kind of issue that gave rise to exclusive federal jurisdiction, a state court may decide it if the defendant raises it as a defense to an action for breach of license. Federal jurisdiction is exclusive only over cases, not questions, arising under the patent laws. Unfortunately, the same arcane criteria define the exclusive authority of the Court of Appeals for the Federal Circuit to review district-court decisions in patent cases under § 1295.

---

[98] 71 U.S. (4 Wall.) 411 (1867).

(ii) Admiralty

Federal district courts have had jurisdiction over admiralty and maritime cases ever since 1789; the present statute is 28 U.S.C. § 1333. In England, admiralty jurisdiction extends only to tidewaters, and the Supreme Court initially construed our statute in accord with this practice. As inland commerce expanded, however, Congress extended admiralty to the Great Lakes and their connecting waters, and the Court upheld it in *The Genesee Chief*[99] in 1851. Congress could not enlarge the constitutional scope of the jurisdiction, the Court said, but its interpretation was persuasive: for all relevant purposes the lakes were like the ocean. Subsequent decisions extended the jurisdiction to other lakes, rivers, and even canals, so long as they constituted part of a continuous water route to other states or nations.

The test of admiralty jurisdiction in contract cases, sensibly enough, has been whether or not the contract is related to maritime commerce. The place the contract was made or to be performed is immaterial. Oddly enough, contracts to build or to sell ships have traditionally been excluded from the jurisdiction, as were ship mortgages until Congress enacted the Ship Mortgage Act, which the Supreme Court upheld in 1934.

---

[99] 53 U.S. 443 (1951)

In tort cases the traditional rule said jurisdiction existed only if the tort occurred on navigable waters. Moreover, as in conventional choice-of-law cases, the tort occurred not where the wrongful act happened but where the victim suffered injury. Thus when a ship collided with a drawbridge, the ship owner could sue in admiralty but the bridge owner could not, since the bridge was an extension of the land.

To remedy this, Congress enacted the Admiralty Extension Act in 1948. The Act extends the jurisdiction to injuries on land caused by a vessel, and lower courts have upheld it, citing *The Genesee Chief*. The Supreme Court, without discussing the validity of the statute, has sensibly held it applicable to harm done by a ship's crew or its cargo as well as by the ship itself.[100] Most recently, *Jerome H. Grubart, Inc. v. Great Lakes Dredge & Dock Co.*[101] applied the Extension Act to uphold admiralty jurisdiction over claims for damage caused when construction equipment on a barge repairing navigational structures in the Chicago River punctured a tunnel and caused basement flooding in downtown Chicago.[102]

---

[100] Gutierrez v. Waterman S.S. Corp., 373 U.S. 206 (1973).

[101] 513 U.S. 527 (1995).

[102] The Extension Act applies only to injuries vessels cause. In cases not involving ships, the shoreline continues to produce arbitrary distinctions. The Sixth Circuit held a suit on behalf of a man who had *fallen* into the water was not maritime because the wrong had occurred when he tripped on the pier; yet when a victim had *dived* from the pier the same court held the tort had not

The courts said the Extension Act did not enlarge federal workers' compensation under the Longshore and Harbor Workers' Compensation Act, which covered only injuries suffered "upon * * * navigable waters." Congress responded by extending compensation to injuries suffered by "maritime" employees on adjoining piers or other areas "customarily used" in servicing vessels, whether or not the ship caused them.

The Supreme Court has extended two seamen's remedies for personal injury shoreward without benefit of statute by classifying them essentially as contractual: Jones Act damages for negligence[103] and maintenance and cure.[104] The Court's refusal to allow tort recovery by a longshoreman injured by his own truck on the pier,[105] however, appeared to end such innovations.

Just the locality test was too narrow to satisfy some purposes of admiralty jurisdiction, for others it was too broad. Finally resolving a conflict, *Executive Jet Aviation, Inc. v. City of Cleveland*[106] refused admiralty jurisdiction over a damage action arising from the crash of an air-

---

occurred until he landed in navigable waters.

[103] O'Donnell v. Great Lakes Dredge & Dock Co., 318 U.S. 36 (1943).

[104] Warren v. United States, 340 U.S. 523 (1951).

[105] Victory Carriers, Inc. v. Law, 404 U.S. 202 (1971).

[106] 409 U.S. 249 (1972).

plane into Lake Erie: a maritime location was insufficient unless the transaction bore "a significant relationship to traditional maritime activity."

In *Offshore Logistics, Inc. v. Tallentire*,[107] however, the Court upheld admiralty jurisdiction over wrongful-death claims arising from the crash of a helicopter carrying workers from an offshore drilling platform. Not only did the Death the High Seas Act, which covers wrongs "occurring on the high seas beyond a marine league from the shore of any state" "expressly provide[ ]" jurisdiction; it also lay under "traditional principles" because the helicopter was "engaging in a function traditionally performed by waterborne vessels." A collision between two pleasure boats is still maritime after *Executive Jet*;[108] an action for injury to shipyard workers exposed to asbestos, according to the courts of appeals, is not.[109]

Admiralty jurisdiction traditionally did not include authority to grant equitable relief. Yet the Supreme Court has upheld Congress's power to authorize equitable remedies in admiralty and sustained the right of a federal court to grant non-statutory equitable relief ancillary to a mari-

---

[107] 277 U.S. 207 (1986).

[108] Foremost Ins. Co. v. Richardson, 457 U.S. 668 (1982).

[109] *E.g.*, Oman v. Johns-Manville Corp., 764 F.3d 224 (4th Cir. 1985).

time claim.[110] The merger of law and admiralty under the Federal Rules of Civil Procedure has helped the lower courts to break down this archaic limitation still further.

Despite § 1333's provision purporting to make federal jurisdiction "exclusive" in admiralty cases, in most instances state courts have concurrent jurisdiction under the next clause: "saving to suitors other remedies to which they are otherwise entitled." The most important exceptions are for *in rem* proceedings, actions for limitation of a ship-owner's liability, and suits against the United States.

Since federal law governs most maritime cases, are they also actions arising under federal law within the meaning of 28 U.S.C. § 1331? One might think the question immaterial; the federal court has jurisdiction in any event under § 1333. The right to jury trial, however, depends upon whether the action lies under § 1331, since (except under the Great Lakes Act) there is no jury in admiralty. Seamen seeking damages for personal injury, therefore, tended to join negligence claims under the Jones Act with claims for unseaworthiness and maintenance and cure under the general maritime law and to argue that the entire case arose under federal law.

---

[110] Swift & Co. Packers v. Compania Colobiana del Caribe, 339 U.S. 684 (1950).

Romero v. International Terminal Operating Co.[111] held it did not. Federal-question jurisdiction, the Court reasoned, existed to provide a forum for vindication of federal rights that had not existed before; § 1333 had already provided a federal forum for claims under the general maritime law. As Justice Brennan observed in a separate opinion, however, the argument proves too much, for a maritime case lies under § 1332 if the parties are from different states; since admiralty jurisdiction overlaps with diversity, there is no reason why it cannot overlap with federal-question jurisdiction as well.

Though *Romero* concluded that jurisdiction over the unseaworthiness and maintenance claims did not lie under § 1331, it did not dismiss them, for jurisdiction under § 1333 was plain. Nor did the Court deny the plaintiff a jury trial on those claims. Since there was a right to jury trial on the Jones Act claim, and since all three claims arose out of the same transaction, trial convenience required a jury decide all of them.[112]

In cases in which there is no Jones Act count to anchor claims under general maritime law, the issue of § 1331 jurisdiction still determines the

---

[111] 358 U.S. 354 (1959).

[112] Fitzgerald v. United States Lines, 374 U.S. 16 (1963). Note the resemblance this device bears to supplemental jurisdiction.

right to a jury. In some cases it determines whether a federal forum is available at all. *Khediuial Line v. Seafarers' International Union*,[113] for example, refused jurisdiction over an action to enjoin picketing a vessel on navigable waters. *Romero* had held that the general maritime law was not a "law[ ] of the United States" within § 1331, so no injunction was available in admiralty. The Ninth Circuit saw it differently, concluding that *Romero* had held only actions that fell within § 1333 were outside § 1331.[114] The latter interpretation tracks *Romero*'s insistence that Congress intended to provide a forum for cases not already within federal authority, but it puts a severe strain on § 1331, for it *requires* the court to find that the general maritime law sometimes is and sometimes is not a "law[ ] of the United States."

Romero may also affect removal from the state courts; despite the broad terms of the removal statute ("any civil action"), the lower courts have generally held, in accord with *Romero* dictum, that cases based solely on § 1333 are not removable.

---

[113] 278 F.2d 49 (2d Cir. 1960).

[114] Marine Cooks & Stewards v. Panama S.S. Co., 265 F.2d 780 (9th Cir. 1959).

(7) Refusals to Exercise Jurisdiction: Abstention

There are times when, although the federal court's jurisdiction is clear, the Supreme Court has nonetheless instructed the lower courts to refuse to exercise it. The refusal is not, as with *forum non conveniens*, because the "geography" is wrong, but for more structural reasons. There are now five or six abstention doctrines (the lines between some of them are not always clear); each has a different conceptual underpinning. All have in common the issue of whether it is appropriate for the federal courts to treat grants of jurisdiction by Congress as "offers they can refuse," because all of the abstention doctrines are judge-made law. Ordinarily, if there is a conflict between common law and a statute, the statute prevails.[115]

(i) *Younger* Abstention

The doctrine long antedates its eponym. Beginning in 1888,[116] the Supreme Court took a dim view of federal courts staying state criminal proceedings. The Court noted, in an apparent bow to the Anti-Injunction Act, that the federal

---

[115] This is subject to the maxim that courts strictly construe statutes in derogation of the common law. With respect to abstention, all of the relevant jurisdictional statutes *preceded* the Court's common-law creation of the doctrines, so the maxim has no force.

[116] *In re* Sawyer, 124 U.S. 200 (1888).

courts' equity jurisdiction extended only to rights of property, not to criminal prosecutions. In its modern incarnation, the doctrine prohibits federal-court interference with pending state criminal prosecutions, whether by injunction,[117] declaratory judgment,[118] or suppression order.[119] The federal plaintiff can avoid abstention only by showing (1) no adequate remedy at law (inability to federal rights by defending a single criminal prosecution[120]) *and* (2) that in the absence of federal intervention, there will be great, immediate, and irreparable harm.[121] Otherwise, the district court must dismiss. The Court grounded its decision on what it called "Our Federalism," and on well-recognized doctrines of equity, comity, and federalism.[122] *Younger* applies as well to courts-martial.[123]

---

[117] Younger v. Harris, 401 U.S. 37 (1971).

[118] Samuels v. Mackel, 401 U.S. 66 (1971).

[119] Perez v. Ledesma, 401 U.S. 82 (1971).

[120] In other words, what the Court referred to as the "cost, anxiety and inconvenience" of defending a single criminal prosecution is *not* great, immediate and irreparable harm.

[121] In one way, *Younger* is a liberalization of the non-interference doctrine. Before *Younger*, federal courts could *never* interfere with a pending state criminal prosecution and could interfere with *threatened* state criminal prosecution only if the plaintiff satisfied the two conditions *Younger* repeated. The *Younger* Court used those two conditions as predicates for interfering with a *pending* state criminal prosecution and explicitly expressed no opinion about circumstances justifying interference with a threatened prosecution.

[122] The Court also held open the possibility that intervention might be appropriate if a state statute were "flagrantly and

Younger was a § 1983 case; its conclusion that a criminal defendant had an adequate opportunity to protect his federal rights in state court seems difficult to square with the premise of § 1983, as emphasized in subsequent cases, that state courts are often inadequate forums for the vindication of federal rights.

(A) *Younger* Ascendant

Following *Younger*, the doctrine expanded along two axes. First, the Court extended it to proceedings other than criminal prosecutions: (1) civil proceedings "in aid of and closely related to criminal statutes * * * ,"[124] (2) any state proceeding in which the state is a party,[125] (3) contempt proceedings in a purely private action,[126] (4) a purely civil state proceeding involving parents alleged to be abusive where there was no single state procedure allowing timely adjudication of the parents' constitutional claims,[127] (5) state administrative proceedings,[128] and finally (6) a purely private lawsuit

---

patently violative of express constitutional prohibitions in every clause, sentence and paragraph, and in whatever manner and against whomever an effort might be made to apply it." Somehow the Court has not yet discovered such a provision.

[123] Schlesinger v. Councilman, 420 U.S. 738 (1975).

[124] Huffman v. Pursue, Ltd., 420 U.S. 592 (1975).

[125] Trainor v. Hernandez, 431 U.S. 434 (1977).

[126] Juidice v. Vail, 430 U.S. 327 (1977).

[127] Moore v. Sims, 442 U.S. 415 (1979).

[128] Ohio Civil Rights Comm'n v. Dayton Christian Sch.,

not involving contempt proceedings.[129] Second, the Court ruled in 1975 that priority of filing means less than one might think. *Hicks v. Miranda*[130] held that *Younger* abstention applies even where the state criminal proceeding commenced *after* the federal litigation, as long as there have been no "proceedings of substance on the merits" in federal court. Denial of a motion for a temporary restraining order was not such a proceeding. It is not clear whether granting a temporary restraining order (which requires the court to have found likelihood of success on the merits) is such a proceeding.

(B) *Younger* Limited

The policy bases of the *Younger* rule help to define its limitations. In *Steffel v. Thompson*,[131] the plaintiff, threatened with arrest for trespass if he continued distributing handbills at a shopping center, sought a declaratory judgment that the state trespass statute was unconstitutional. The Court held that *Younger* was no bar. No prosecution had begun, so there was no danger of duplicating or disrupting state-court proceedings. For the same rea-

---

Inc., 477 U.S. 619 (1986).

[129] Pennzoil Company v. Texaco, Inc., 481 U.S. 1 (1987).

[130] 422 U.S. 332 (1975).

[131] 415 U.S. 452 (1974). *Steffel* avoided potential ripeness problems because Steffel's companion did continue distributing handbills and was arrested. Most situations, however, do not have a "control case."

son, defense against state prosecution was a wholly inadequate remedy: "[A] refusal on the part of the federal courts to intervene * * * may place the hapless plaintiff between the Scylla of intentionally flouting state law and the Charybdis of foregoing what he believes to be constitutionally protected activity." Note, though, the possible effect of *Hicks v. Miranda* on the apparent *Steffel* exception.

In *Doran v. Salem Inn*,[132] the Court added that, while normally a declaratory judgment removed the necessity for enjoining a threatened prosecution, the *Steffel* principle permitted *preliminary* injunctions because there is no declaratory alternative for maintaining the *status quo*. But the crux of the question is whether leaving the federal plaintiff to defend a state prosecution would subject him to the risk of serious and irreparable harm, not simply whether a state prosecution is pending when the federal suit begins. Thus, if there is an agreement not to prosecute for future violations until the conclusion of a contemplated test prosecution, the Court has found no need for federal intervention. One might think, in light of the preliminary relief in *Doran,* that even a pending state prosecution affords inadequate protection to a federal plaintiff seeking assurance that sim-

---

[132] 421 U.S. 927 (1975).

ilar future conduct was protected. *Roe v. Wade*,[133] however, held the contrary.

Most recently, a unanimous Court ruled that *Younger* does not extend to purely civil suits that do not implicate state judicial systems. The Court characterized the *Younger* as limited to (1) state criminal cases, (2) certain civil enforcement proceedings, and (3) other civil proceedings on orders "uniquely in furtherance" of state courts' ability to perform judicial functions. *Sprint Communications, Inc. v. Jacobs*[134] viewed these three categories as "exceptional" and strongly suggested that they fully describe the limits of *Younger* abstention.

(ii) *Pullman* Abstention

In *Railroad Commission v. Pullman Co.*,[135] the Pullman Company challenged a state administrative order on grounds of racial discrimination under both federal and state law. The order required conductors (all of whom were white) rather than porters (all of whom were black) to be in charge of all sleeping cars. The Court articulated a three-part test for abstention: (1) the case presents questions of federal constitutional law and state law, (2) the resolution of the state-law questions is unclear, *and* (3) resolution of

---

[133] 410 U.S. 113 (1973).

[134] 134 S. Ct. 584 (2013).

[135] 312 U.S. 496 (1941).

the state-law questions may make it unnecessary to adjudicate the federal constitutional issues.[136] The Court ordered the federal district court to retain the case pending the parties going to state court for an interpretation of state law, which might have allowed Pullman to prevail.[137] Note that this differs from *Younger* abstention. *Younger* requires dismissing the federal action; *Pullman* may only cause delay.

A statute may be too clear to require state-court interpretation. If there is only one reasonable interpretation, there is no need to send the parties to the state courts. It is also possible for a statute to be vague in a way that would require multiple state adjudications to clarify it, and the federal court will not abstain in that circumstance either.[138]

The paradigm case for *Pullman* abstention is a suit to enjoin a state officer on federal constitutional grounds from enforcing ambiguous state law. *Pullman* applies to civil-rights cases under 42 U.S.C. § 1983, notwithstanding the mistrust

---

[136] The Court later ruled that abstention might be appropriate if the interpretation of state law might significantly change the nature of the constitutional question rather than eliminating it completely. Harrison v. NAACP, 360 U.S. 167 (1959).

[137] If Texas law would have disapproved the rule, there would be no need to decide any constitutional issue.

[138] *See* Baggett v. Bullitt, 377 U.S. 360 (1964) (statute requiring teachers to "by precept and example promote respect for the flag and the institutions of the United States * * *).

of state courts that § 1983's correlate jurisdictional statute, 28 U.S.C. § 1343, connotes[139] and that the Court has stressed in arguably analogous cases. Even suits that the United States brings may be candidates for abstention.

Perhaps troubled by the tension between abstention and the jurisdictional grant, the Court set limits in *England v. Louisiana State Board of Medical Examiners*.[140] When the federal court abstains, the parties submit only the state-law questions to the state court for decision; they reserve federal questions for later federal decision in the event that the constitutional question remains and requires decision after resolution of the state-law issues. The parties must *inform* the state court of the constitutional issues, because that may affect the state court's interpretation of state law.

England blunts some of the objections to *Pullman* but does not entirely eliminate them. Sections 1331 and 1343 give jurisdiction over the entire action, not merely the federal questions it contains. When there is also diversity jurisdiction, abstention denies the out-of-state litigant protection from state-court bias. Abstention also splits what ought to be a single case between two forums. That is an uneconom-

---

[139] Congress, though vesting the jurisdiction in 1871, notably did not make it exclusive.

[140] 375 U.S. 411 (1964).

ical use of court, attorney, and litigant resources and significantly delays vindicating federal rights. When an appellate federal court rules that the district court should have abstained rather than trying the case on the merits, the process of referring state-law issues to the state court and later returning to federal court can take years.

Abstention is not automatic even when resolution of unclear state law can avoid a substantial constitutional question. For example, in *Pike v. Bruce Church, Inc.*,[141] delay in determining whether a state statute could constitutionally apply to a particular transaction would have resulted in loss of $700,000; the Court refused abstention "in view of the emergency situation presented, and the fact that only a narrow and specific application of the Act was challenged." The Court has also declined abstention when the unclear state law "mirrors" a provision (such as the Equal Protection Clause) of the federal Constitution.[142]

Pullman abstention has waned, as more states have enacted statutes allowing federal courts to certify unclear issues of state law to the state's highest court. Certification saves time and expense otherwise necessarily involved in the *Pullman* procedure. All states other than

---

[141] 397 U.S. 137 (1970).

[142] Examining Bd. v. Flores de Otero, 426 U.S. 572 (1976).

North Carolina now have certification statutes. Most permit certification only where the state issue is determinative and there is no controlling precedent.

Certification statutes vary. Some states will accept certification from any federal court; others only from appellate federal courts. In the latter states, district courts presumably order *Pullman* abstention more frequently than courts in states that allow district-court certification.[143] A fair number of state statutes also permit certification from other states' courts and from foreign courts.

(iii)   *Burford* Abstention

Occasional decisions have gone beyond *Pullman* by ordering dismissal of suits challenging state-administrative-agency determinations even in the absence of any suggestion that state law was unclear. The best known, *Burford v. Sun Oil* Co.,[144] declined to review an order granting a permit to drill for oil, invoking "the nonlegal complexity" of the state's oil-conservation scheme, the "great public importance" of the subject, and the state's policy of promoting uniformity of decision by centralizing review in a single court. *Alabama Public Service*

---

[143] Abstention orders are not appealable interlocutory orders as of right under 28 U.S.C. § 1292, but the circuit courts have discretion to hear them.

[144] 319 U.S. 315 (1943).

Comm. v. Southern Ry.,[145] ordered dismissal of a suit challenging the refusal to permit abandonment of a short interstate rail route because the constitutional question was "local" and because Alabama, like Texas in *Burford,* had attempted to centralize judicial review.

Burford abstention is rare. For example, the Court has never forbidden federal courts to examine state administrative orders in ordinary welfare or school-segregation cases. *Quackenbush v. Allstate Ins. Co.*[146] held that *Burford* abstention is never appropriate in suits seeking only damages, despite the Court's earlier extension[147] of the Tax Injunction Act's clear prohibition of injunctions against collection of state taxes to actions seeking only damages.

(iv)   *Colorado River*[148] Abstention

If for no other reason, this case would be remarkable because the United States invoked the federal courts' jurisdiction pursuant to 28 U.S.C. § 1345, and the Supreme Court nonetheless directed abstention. There was parallel litigation over water rights in state and federal courts. The Court noted that the case did not fit within

---

[145] 341 U.S. 341 (1951).

[146] 517 U.S. 706 (1996).

[147] Fair Assessment in Real Estate Ass'n v. McNary, 454 U.S. 100 (1981).

[148] Colorado River Water Comm'n v. United States, 424 U.S. 800 (1976).

the *Pullman*, *Younger*, or *Burford* abstention doctrines. While paying lip service to "the virtually unflagging obligation of the federal courts to exercise the jurisdiction given them * * * ," the Court nonetheless "flagged" the obligation just a bit more. It noted (1) the undesirability of piecemeal adjudication of water rights, (2) the existence of a unified, ongoing system of water rights adjudication, (3) the government's participation in it in many districts, (4) the absence of any significant proceedings in the federal court (a faint echo, perhaps, of *Hicks v. Miranda*), and (5) the geographical inconvenience of litigants having to travel 300 miles to the federal court. Those factors combined to make abstention appropriate.

(v) *Thibodaux* Abstention

As a rule, abstention is inappropriate in diversity cases.[149] *Pullman* abstention unavailable, and the Court has ruled that abstaining simply because there are unclear issues of state law contravenes Congress's intent that federal courts hear diversity cases to avoid the possibility or perception of local bias. However, eminent domain cases are "special" because they are "intimately involved with sovereign prerogative" and so sometimes justify abstention.[150]   And

---

[149] Meredith v. City of Winter Haven, 320 U.S. 228 (1943).

[150] Louisiana Power & Light Co. v. City of Thibodaux, 360 U.S. 25, 28 (1959).

sometimes they don't.[151]   The Court was fragmented in those two decisions, announced on the same day. In *Thibadaux*, there were unclear issues of state law; in *Frank Mashuda* there were not. The Court has since distinguished the cases not on that basis, but because one case merely stayed the federal action (abstention permitted) while the other dismissed it. Yet the Court has made clear that ambiguity of state law is not enough to support abstention; there must be in addition either an unusually strong state interest, as in *Thibodaux*, or a substantial constitutional question that a state court decision may avoid or significantly change by deciding the state-law question. The status of *Thibodaux* abstention remains unclear.

B. Article I Courts

The Constitution is conspicuously silent about any federal judicial system outside of Article III. "Court" appears only in three places: (1) Article III, (2) Article I, § 8, cl. 9—giving Congress the power "to constitute tribunals inferior to the supreme Court"—an unambiguous reference to the language of Article III, and (3) Article II, § 2, cl. 2—giving the president the power to appoint federal judges subject to the Senate's advice and consent. One searches in vain for congressional authority to create non-

---

[151] Allegheny County v. Frank Mashuda Co., 360 U.S. 185 (1959).

Article-III courts and staff them with judges who do not have the salary and tenure protections that Article III mandates for judges appointed under that Article.

Nonetheless, Congress has created "legislative courts"—federal courts on which judges (known as "Article I judges") sit for fixed terms and lack Article III protections. Legislative courts exist basically in three areas: (1) for lands having no state sovereign, such as territories and the District of Columbia, (2) military courts, and (3) courts for "public rights" cases—cases for which Congress need provide no judicial process at all.[152] These three categories are not quite exhaustive, however.

For example, Congress created the Court of Customs Appeals. The Supreme Court held that the court could exercise non-Article-III judicial authority because Congress acted under its Article-I power to lay and collect taxes rather than under Article III.[153] Since Congress could have

---

[152] The Court originally limited public-rights cases to those in which the government was a party, but abandoned that requirement in Granfinanciera, S.A. v. Nordberg, 492 U.S. 33 (1989), holding that when a bankruptcy trustee sued to recover allegedly fraudulently transferred assets, the defendants, who had not submitted a claim against the bankrupt's estate, were entitled to a jury trial. The action was clearly a core proceeding, and could proceed in the Bankruptcy Court, but Congress's specification of non-jury trials in Bankruptcy Court violated the Seventh Amendment as applied.

[153] Ex parte Bakelite Corp., 279 U.S. 438 (1929).

mandated collection of customs duties without any judicial process, the Court ruled that it could take the lesser step of creating a court for this purpose without the protections of Article III.

The argument is questionable. Summary seizure of property generally offends due process.[154] Even where it does not, the Court demands an opportunity for subsequent redress.[155] The Court's conclusion in *Bakelite* ignores the plain language of Article III. The Constitution does not require creating inferior federal courts, but it flatly demands that federal judges have tenure during good behavior and irreducible salaries.

Bakelite did not break down the tenure requirement entirely. The Court noted that "legislative" courts could have jurisdiction only over cases involving "public rights" to which the government was a party, though the latter factor is

---

[154] *See, e.g.*, North Georgia Finishing, Inc. v. Di-Chem, 419 U.S. 601 (1975) (prejudgment garnishment order issued by court clerk based on summary affidavit and without possibility of early hearing denied due process); Fuentes v. Shevin, 407 U.S. 67 (1972) (prejudgment replevin statutes allowing seizure of chattels without prior hearing denied due process); Sniadach v. Family Fin. Corp., 395 U.S. 337 (1969) (prejudgment garnishment freezing defendant's wages pending trial with no opportunity for prior hearing denied due process);

[155] *See, e.g.*, Mitchell v. W.T. Grant Co., 416 U.S. 600 (1974) (*ex parte* writ of sequestration to prevent waste or alienation of encumbered property and allowing immediate post-seizure hearing not denial of due process).

no longer imperative. "Inherently judicial" controversies (whatever they might be) were only for Article III courts.

Crowell v. Benson[156] further undermined Article III's requirements. Congress established an administrative tribunal to rule on maritime workers' compensation claims. A claimant argued that Article III required *de novo* review[157] of issues of fact. The Court agreed with respect to facts the Court deemed to be both jurisdictional and constitutional, such as whether the plaintiff was an employee and whether the injury occurred in navigable waters. Other facts required no such intensive reexamination. Thus, after *Crowell*, the administrative agency could make factual determinations subject only to limited judicial oversight even in a case that clearly was inherently judicial—a private controversy over compensation for personal injury. The Article-III requirements of life tenure and irreducible salary for judges "both of the supreme and inferior courts" appears to apply only to judges of the district, circuit and Supreme courts.

Northern Pipeline Construction Co. v. Marathon Pipeline Co.[158] seemed to give new life to

---

[156] 285 U.S. 22 (1932).

[157] *"De novo* review" is a misnomer. This "review" is the appellate body considering the matter afresh, constrained by nothing other than whatever uncompelled deference it may choose to accord the tribunal from which the appeal comes.

[158] 458 U.S. 50 (1982).

the Article-III requirements when it struck down a statute that entrusted the bankruptcy jurisdiction of district courts to bankruptcy judges serving fourteen-year terms. The Court split five to four; there was no majority opinion. The plurality ruled that the only "exceptions" from Article III were territorial and military courts and courts dealing with public rights matters.

The dissent characterized the matter differently. Seizing on the plurality's concession that Congress could create Article I courts for "all rights and duties arising under otherwise valid federal laws," it argued that there was no good reason to excluding bankruptcy cases. Even disputes about the bankrupt's estate resting on state law had long been part of bankruptcy procedure that included (before the 1978 amendments to the bankruptcy code) preliminary determinations by referees, who certainly were not Article-III judges. The dissent thought that the ability to appeal bankruptcy court determinations to Article-III courts was sufficient.

Northern Pipeline did not end the discussion. Four years later, the Court changed two areas of Article-I-court doctrine.[159] Previously, the Court had viewed the Article-III protections only as separation-of-powers concerns, but the Justices

---

[159] Commodity Futures Trading Comm'n v. Schor, 478 U.S. 833 (1986).

now discerned a litigant's right to have Article-III judges as insulation from undue influence from the other branches. That right, like other constitutional rights, is waivable, but even if the litigants waive, the structural separation-of-powers concern remains.

The second change was the Court's apparent shift from a categorical approach to Article-I courts to a balancing approach, similar to what Justice White had urged in his *Northern Pipeline* dissent but with additional consideration of the origin of the underlying rights. Private-rights cases presumptively have to go to Article-III courts, but the litigant-waiver possibility and the fact that Congress did *not* withdraw jurisdiction from the district courts, make Article-I adjudication permissible because parties consent to it. The underlying concern about the legitimacy of Article-I courts in light of Article III remains.

Today, the district courts have original and exclusive jurisdiction over bankruptcy (28 U.S.C. § 1334) and may refer such cases to a bankruptcy judge. Bankruptcy law permits bankruptcy judges to render final judgments in "core proceedings," and includes a non-exhaustive list of examples. The district courts hear appeals from such judgments. Bankruptcy judges may also hear non-core claims, but the judges only submit proposed findings of fact and conclusions of law to the district court rather than making a final adjudication.

In *Stern v. Marshall*,[160] someone asserted a defamation claim against the bankrupt in the bankruptcy proceeding, and the bankrupt counterclaimed for tortious interference with an anticipated gift. The counterclaim was within the statutory language defining core proceedings, and the party asserting the defamation claim not only failed to object to adjudication, but explicitly affirmed that he was content to have the bankruptcy court exercise jurisdiction. (He became less content after the bankruptcy court dismissed the defamation claim and awarded the bankrupt a multimillion dollar judgment on the counterclaim.)

The Court was unanimous that the counterclaim was a core proceeding within the meaning of the bankruptcy statute, but split five-four on the result. The majority ruled that the counterclaim was not within any of the three categories of cases Article-I judges could adjudicate (noting that it was not a public rights case "by any definition"). Therefore, the bankruptcy statute provision apparently authorizing adjudication was unconstitutional as applied. The dissent accused the majority of undermining *Crowell v. Benson*'s well-established law, but what really separated the Justices appeared to be that the majority stayed with the Court's previous, cate-

---

[160] 131 S. Ct. 2594 (2011).

gorical approach, whereas the dissent preferred a more pragmatic approach.

V. APPELLATE AND COLLATERAL REVIEW

A. Paths to Review

1. Appeal, Certiorari, and Certification

Originally the Supreme Court's entire jurisdiction was mandatory. The appellate procedural device was a "writ of error," though in 1928 Congress replaced the writ of error with review by appeal (also mandatory). Increasing burdens on the Court have led Congress progressively to reduce mandatory jurisdiction, substituting the discretionary writ of certiorari. The Court's appellate jurisdiction is now almost entirely discretionary; a petitioner for certiorari must persuade at least four Justices that the Court should hear the case. The remaining exception is 28 U.S.C. § 1253, which provides mandatory appeal from three-judge district courts, principally in actions to enjoin legislative apportionments on constitutional grounds.

In addition to the appeal and certiorari jurisdiction, § 1254 empowers the Supreme Court to decide questions of law the courts of appeals certify to it. The statute looks permissive. Commentators tend to say the Court must review, but the Court has developed limiting rules. For example, *Wisniewski v. United States*[161] held that courts of appeals should not certify ques-

---

[161] 353 U.S. 901 (1957).

tions merely to resolve a conflict among different panels of their own judges. In general, the Court added, it was the job of the court of appeals to decide its own cases, not to pass the buck. Certification is rarely proper, permissible if when the identical question is already pending before the Supreme Court or if (as in Mississippi Governor Ross Barnett's demand for a jury trial in a contempt case), the court of appeals itself was equally divided and there was no lower court opinion to affirm. Interestingly, the *per curiam* opinion finished by saying that the certificate "must" be dismissed. Since the courts of appeals rarely used certification, Congress, when it last extensively revised the Judicial Code (in 1948), seriously considered abolishing it. Three Justices testified that certification was a good practice, and it remains on the books.

2. The Final Judgment Rule—Generally

Interlocutory appeals interrupt ongoing proceedings, burden appellate courts, and often delay ultimate resolution of disputes. Section 1291 provides appeal from "final decisions" of the district courts; § 1257 authorizes the Supreme Court to review "final judgments" of state tribunals.

Thus, while grant of a motion to dismiss for failure to state a claim terminates the case and is therefore appealable, denial contemplates further trial-level proceedings, and there is normally no appeal. Similarly, when a trial court denies a motion for a new trial, the court enters a final (appealable) judgment. But if the court grants the motion, proceedings in the trial court are not over, so in most cases there is no immediate appeal.

However, on occasion interlocutory appeal can save time or prevent irreparable harm, and Congress has made several exceptions to the final-judgment rule. For example, § 1292(a), allows immediate review of many interlocutory federal orders respecting injunctions. Grant or denial of a preliminary injunction may effectively decide the merits in many cases, and only immediate review can avoid irreparable harm.

Section 1292(b) authorizes a federal district judge to certify for interlocutory appeal any "controlling" and debatable issue of law whose immediate decision "may materially advance the termination of the litigation." F.R.C.P. Rule 54(b) permits additional interlocutory appeals by allowing trial judges to enter judgment on individual claims in a case before resolving the rest of it if the district judge believes there is no just reason for delay. The courts of appeals need not entertain the appeal.

The All Writs Act, 28 U.S.C. § 1651, allows appellate courts to issue writs of mandamus or prohibition where "necessary or appropriate in aid of" their own jurisdiction. *La Buy v. Howes Leather Co.*[162] rejected the argument that this provision only allowed the appellate court to prevent being ousted of jurisdiction (*e.g.*, by transfer of the case to another circuit). The in-aid-of-jurisdiction requirement applies whenever the appellate court could ultimately review a final judgment. Nevertheless, in order not to undermine the general policy against piecemeal appeals, the Court has made clear that these writs are available only in exceptional cases. Mandamus or prohibition most likely lies only when the lower-court order "was made without jurisdiction, * * * is characteristic of an erroneous practice likely to reoccur, * * * [or] exemplifies a novel and important question in need of guidelines for the future resolution of similar cases."

Section 1254 permits the Supreme Court to review court-of-appeals cases at any time. This not only allows review of interlocutory court-of-appeals orders, but also allows the Court to bypass the court of appeals entirely by taking a case as soon as it reaches the appellate court. Supreme Court Rule 11 reserves this for cases of "imperative public importance." The Court did so

---

[162] 352 U.S. 249 (1957).

in the steel seizure case[163] and in *United States v. Nixon*,[164] which involved the Watergate tapes. Yet the Court refused certiorari before judgment in the court of appeals in the Little Rock segregation case,[165] which one might have thought presented comparable urgency, and it has granted immediate review, usually in order to consolidate cases presenting similar issues, in cases of no great urgency at all.

It is not always obvious whether a decision or judgment is "final" for purposes of appeal, and the Supreme Court has severely watered down the requirement in recent years as applied to both state and federal decisions. Discussion of those more specialized variations in the final-judgment rule appears at pages 138, 143, and 143.

B. Supreme Court Review of State Court Decisions

1. Federal and State Issues

Section 25 of the Judiciary Act of 1789 provided Supreme Court review of state-court decisions, but only when a claim of federal right had been denied in the court below—the situation in

---

[163] Youngstown Sheet & Tube Co. v. Sawyer, 343 U.S. 579 (1952).

[164] 418 U.S. 683 (1974).

[165] Aaron v. Cooper, 357 U.S. 566 (1958).

which a state judgment could have the greatest adverse effect on federal policy. All review under § 25 was "as of right." In 1914, Congress extended the statute to cases in which a state court had upheld a federal right, but provided review only by certiorari, not by writ of error. Today, 28 U.S.C. § 1257 authorizes review of state-court judgments in all cases involving federal law.[166] Review lies from "the highest court of a State in which a decision could be had," which is not always the highest court in the state. If the state's highest court declines discretionary review, or if state law provides no appeal within the state system, Supreme Court review by certiorari is available. The most famous "jump" occurred in *Thompson v. City of Louisville*,[167] when the Supreme Court reviewed the judgment of the Louisville Police Court (no appeal being permitted within the Kentucky judicial system) convicting Thompson of loitering and disorderly conduct.

Martin v. Hunter's Lessee[168] upheld § 25. Virginia confiscated land owned by a British

---

[166] This is not as clear as might be. Section 1257 does not appear to authorize review of cases where the petitioner attacks a state common-law rule as violating supremacy or where a state court misinterprets or misapplies a federal common-law rule.

[167] 362 U.S. 199 (1960).

[168] 14 U.S. (1 Wheat.) 304 (1816).

subject; on an earlier appeal the Court had held that offended a treaty. The state court refused to obey the mandate, arguing that the Supreme Court could not constitutionally review a state-court decision. The Supreme Court reversed again, relying in part upon the constitutional text: Article III extended the judicial power to "all" cases arising under the Constitution, and some such cases were in state courts. Supreme Court review of state courts was necessary to achieve the constitutional provision's purposes to protect federal rights and ensure the uniformity of federal law.

Murdock v. City of Memphis[169] held that the Court's power to review state-court judgments extends only to federal questions forming part or all of the basis for the judgments. Supreme Court review of state-law decisions is unnecessary either to vindicate federal rights or to promote uniformity, and it would significantly impair the states' power to define their own laws. Thus, there is no supplemental jurisdiction over state issues when the Supreme Court reviews a state-court judgment, and no need for it either. Turning away the state claim does not cause multiple litigation; the state court has already adjudicated the claim.

---

[169] 87 U.S. (20 Wall.) 590 (1875)

The opinion did one additional thing, which acts as a corollary to the Court's jurisdiction to review state-court decisions. If the state court's judgment rests on an adequate and independent state ground, the Supreme Court should not disturb the state-court judgment even if the state court misapprehended federal law. *Murdock* prescribed a seven-step inquiry for reviewing state court opinions. By "adequate and independent," the Court meant that overturning the state court's ruling on the federal law would have no effect on the result of the case. This may sound like the very definition of an advisory opinion,[170] but in *Murdock*'s sequence, deciding whether the state court ruled correctly on the federal law came before deciding whether, even if the state court was wrong, there was nonetheless an adequate and independent state ground.

Murdock found the state court's ruling on the federal-law issue was correct and affirmed the judgment. Later Courts inverted the inquiry sequence. Today, if there is an adequate and independent state ground, the Court dismisses for lack of jurisdiction. The hard work is determining whether the state ground is both adequate and independent.

---

[170] It certainly when the state-law ground is substantive; when it is procedural, the picture becomes muddied. *See infra* at pages 123-127.

2. Adequate and Independent State Grounds of Substantive Law

a. Clearly Adequate State Grounds

"Adequacy" is a question of federal law. But for the unfortunate sequence, *Murdock* could have been a perfect example of an adequate state ground. The dispute arose in 1854, but the action did not begin until long after the state statute of limitations had expired. State law thus made the action untimely. The issue of federal law was whether a conveyance of land from the United States to Memphis included the land being held in trust for the descendants of the original grantor, who donated land to Memphis with restrictions. The state court held that the conveyance from the United States neither included nor was subject to any trust. Examining the state court's opinions makes clear that the court did not base its decision on the limitations point. Had it done so, its decision of the federal issue, whether correct or not, would have been irrelevant to the disposition of the case because of the limitations problem. Even had the Supreme Court ruled that the state court erred on the federal question, the state court's dismissal of the action as untimely would have stood. The Court's opinion would have been purely advisory.

Fox Film Co. v. Muller[171] provided an actual example and corrected the sequence of inquiry. An earlier Supreme Court case had declared invalid (under the Sherman Antitrust Act) an arbitration clause that was a standard part of every movie exhibitor's contract. Muller had prevailed in the state courts on that basis, and the state's highest court had ruled that the offending clause was not severable from the remainder of the contract. The Supreme Court, in those pre-*Erie* days, found the severability issue one of "general and not of federal law."[172] The Court rejected Fox Film's argument that severability was a question of federal law and ruled that there was then a non-federal ground sufficient to sustain the state court's judgment. It dismissed the writ "for want of jurisdiction."

This does not mean that the Supreme Court can never review a judgment based on both federal and state grounds. When a state court concludes that its law violates *neither* the federal nor the state constitution, a decision that the law does violate the federal Constitution requires reversal because the state ground is not adequate to sustain the judgment. Whether the Court has jurisdiction depends entirely upon whether its deci-

---

[171] 296 U.S. 207 (1935).

[172] Today the Court would say "state law."

sion of the federal question may affect the result reached by the court below.

When the state court rules on both state and federal grounds, one must consider three sub-categories. First, there are cases in which the state ground is clearly adequate and independent, precluding Supreme Court review. In *Jankovich v. Indiana Toll Road Commission*,[173] the Indiana Supreme Court found that a city airport zoning ordinance that sharply limited the permissible height of structures on land adjacent to the airport violated both the state and federal constitutions. The Court granted certiorari but dismissed the writ as improvidently granted upon finding that Indiana law defined usable air space above private property as part of the property and that the ordinance effectively took that property with no compensation. The Indiana Supreme Court's opinion, while not discussing the Indiana constitutional issue separately from the Fourteenth Amendment issue, explicitly relied on Indiana law. A Supreme Court determination that the ordinance did not offend the federal Constitution, therefore, would not have affected the result; the ordinance would still have been invalid under the state constitu-

---

[173] 379 U.S. 487 (1965).

tion. Deciding the federal question would have yielded an advisory opinion.

b. Not Clearly Adequate State Grounds

Two Justices dissented in *Jankovich*, arguing that the lower court's opinion was at least ambiguous about the basis for the decision and that the Court should remand for clarification. That brings us to the second subcategory: cases where the state court's basis for decision is unclear. The Court now deals with such cases in two ways. Originally, the Court recognized prescribed remand in three circumstances: (1) where changes in state law subsequent to the state court's judgment might affect the disposition of the case, (2) where the record did not clearly reflect the facts underlying the federal issue, and (3) where the actual ground—state or federal—for the state court's decision was not clear.[174] The first two occasions survive today, but the Court has dispensed with the third—sometimes.[175]

---

[174] Minnesota v. Nat'l Tea Co., 309 U.S. 551 (1940).

[175] *But see* Bush v. Palm Beach County Canvassing Bd., 531 U.S. 70 (2000). The Court did remand for clarification of the precise basis for the decision. The *per curiam* Court cited *National Tea* and did not so much as mention *Michigan v. Long*, discussed in the next paragraph. Of course, the sibling case, Bush v. Gore, 531 U.S. 98 (2000), gets most of the attention.

Michigan v. Long[176] established a new presumption where the state court's ground for decision might have been either state or federal. The opinion recited the majority's dissatisfaction with the Court's previous approaches of dismissing outright (on the theory that the party invoking the Court's jurisdiction has the burden to demonstrate its existence), remanding for clarification from the state court, or continuing the case so that counsel could return to the state court to seek clarification. Disapproving such procedures as *ad hoc* and "antithetical to the doctrinal consistency that is required when sensitive issues of federal-state relations are involved," the Court announced a new approach.

> Accordingly, when, as in this case, a state court decision fairly appears to rest primarily on federal law, or to be interwoven with the federal law, and when the adequacy and independence of any possible state law ground is not clear from the face of the opinion, we will accept as the most reasonable explanation that the state court decided the case the way it did because it believed that federal law required it to do so. If a state court chooses merely to

---

[176] 463 U.S. 1032 (1983).

rely on federal precedents as it would on the precedents of all other jurisdictions, then it need only make clear by a plain statement in its judgment or opinion that the federal cases are being used only for the purpose of guidance, and do not themselves compel the result that the court has reached. In this way, both justice and judicial administration will be greatly improved. If the state court decision indicates clearly and expressly that it is alternatively based on *bona fide* separate, adequate, and independent grounds, we, of course, will not undertake to review the decision.

The state courts have accepted the invitation. The Oregon Supreme Court announced an opinion the same day that *Michigan v. Long* came down, and one might view its words as a judicial declaration of independence:

This court like others has high respect for the opinions of the Supreme Court, particularly when they provide insight into the origins of provisions common to the state and federal bills of rights rather than only a contemporary "balance" of pragmatic considerations about which reasonable people may differ over time and among the several states. It is therefore to be expected that counsel and courts often will refer to federal decisions, or to commentary based on such decisions, even in debating an undecided issue under state law. Lest there be any doubt about it, when this court cites federal opinions in interpreting a provision of Oregon law, it does so because it finds the views there expressed persuasive, not because it considers itself bound to do so by its understanding of federal doctrines.[177]

The state court wrote that language after the United States Supreme Court had remanded the case for further proceedings, specifically finding that there was *no* adequate independent state ground. On remand, the intermediate state court specified that its decision rested on state law and affirmed the conviction. The Oregon Supreme Court affirmed, first delivering the quoted verbal slap to the United States Supreme Court. Other states have echoed Oregon's sentiments.[178]

---

[177] State v. Kennedy, 666 P.2d 1316 (Or. 1983).

[178] On perhaps a less strident note, consider Wyoming's Supreme Court: "The decision of this court is based on an adequate and independent state ground[,] and any reference to federal law is for illustrative purposes only and in no way compels the result obtained." Rocky Mountain Oil and Gas Ass'n v.

c. Independent State Grounds

The third subcategory of cases where the state court cited both federal and state law in its decision involves independence. Independence is not entirely separate from adequacy. A state ground for decision that is not independent of federal law cannot be adequate. *Delaware v. Prouse*[179] concluded that the search-and-seizure provision in Delaware's constitution provided no greater protection than the Fourth Amendment and that "the Delaware Supreme Court did not intend to rest its decision independently on the State Constitution and that we have jurisdiction in this case." *Prouse* perhaps anticipated *Long*'s approach—without the uncertainty—but the Court's analysis in reaching that conclusion was less than persuasive.

Noting that the Delaware Supreme Court had previously stated that any violation of the Fourth Amendment necessarily violated the Delaware constitution's cognate provision, the Court declined to find the Delaware provision independent. There is less to this observation than meets the eye. All the Delaware court's statement recognized was the Supremacy Clause. If that part

---

State Bd. of Equalization, 749 P.2d 221, 233 n.15 (Wyo. 1988) (citing *Long*).

[179] 440 U.S. 648 (1979).

of the statement were not true, the Delaware constitutional provision would have been unconstitutional because of U.S. CONST. art. VI, § 2, combined with the Fourth Amendment. But in the
same statement, the Delaware Supreme Court
described the Delaware provision as "substantially similar to the Fourth Amendment"—a
much sounder basis for the U.S. Supreme
Court's conclusion about independence though
not one upon which the Court seemed to place
much emphasis.

Other states, however, have explicitly said
that state constitutional provisions mirroring
federal constitutional language nonetheless provide broader protection to the individual. In
such a circumstance, the U.S. Supreme Court
has no jurisdiction to review. States are at liberty to circumscribe state officials' power more
strictly than does the U.S. Constitution, thus
giving more protection to the individual; they
merely cannot give less protection.

d. State Incorporation of Federal Law; Federal Incorporation of State Law

States sometimes adopt federal law by reference, and sometimes the reference is oblique.
When California exempted from a motor vehicle
fuel tax "the government of the United States or

any department thereof,"[180] it implicitly adopted the federal law regarding whether a particular entity was a "department." The Court held that state adoption of federal law as a state standard was perfectly permissible, but the state had to be correct in its interpretation of the federal law. The Court had jurisdiction to review. In effect, the Court said that federal law does not lose its federal character merely because of adoption by a state.

In the converse case, when federal law adopts state law (as where a federal statute refers to "personal property" but does not define it),[181] the state's definition is authoritative *unless* the state has discriminated against the federal government or violated some provision of federal law. The Court reasoned that by not defining the term, Congress intended state rules to govern. The state rules become, effectively, federal common law, albeit common law to which the states give content.

e. Review of Findings of Fact—Sham Findings

Appellate courts, especially the Supreme Court, only rarely (and narrowly) review findings of fact.

---

[180] Standard Oil v. Johnson, 316 U.S. 481 (1942).

[181] Reconstruction Fin. Corp. v. Beaver County, 328 U.S. 204 (1946).

Sometimes a state court has made findings of fact not justified by the record, to insulate the case from Supreme Court review. In one famous case, county taxing authorities asserted the power to tax property owned by Native Americans that was exempt from state taxation. The authorities demanded payment and threatened to seize and sell the properties if the owners did not pay and to asses substantial penalties if the owners paid late. The owners, having already launched a state judicial challenge, paid the taxes under protest. The state supreme court overturned a plaintiffs' victory and found that as a matter of state law the owners had paid the taxes "voluntarily." The United States Supreme Court declined to dismiss, determining that the county's demurrer to the complaint rendered the state supreme court's finding of voluntary payment "without any fair or substantial support," and reversed.[182] The Court extended that approach to cases where a conviction rested upon an inference unsupportable from the evidence[183] and to a situation where the Court found that one of the parties had acted fraudulently in belatedly including the names of black citizens on an otherwise all-white jury roll.[184]

---

[182] Ward v. Board of County Comm'rs, 253 U.S. 17 (1920).

[183] Fiske v. Kansas, 274 U.S. 380 (1927).

[184] Norris v. Alabama, 294 U.S. 587 (1935).

3. Adequate and Independent State Grounds of Procedural Law

Henry v. Mississippi[185] illustrates the adequate-state-ground doctrine in a procedural context. The Mississippi Supreme Court acknowledged that the trial court admitted illegally obtained evidence in a criminal trial. However, there was no reversal because Henry failed to object, as state law required, when the prosecution offered the evidence. The question was whether the state-law ground was adequate.

The adequate-state-ground doctrine, Justice Brennan argued, functions differently when the state law is procedural:

> Where the ground involved is substantive, the determination of the federal question cannot affect the disposition if the state court decision on the state law question is allowed to stand * * * . A procedural default which is held to bar challenge to a conviction in state courts * * * prevents implementation of the federal right * * * . [W]hen and how defaults in compliance with state procedural rules can preclude our consideration of a federal question is itself a federal question.

---

[185] 379 U.S. 443 (1965).

The real question in *Henry* was whether the state ground was unconstitutional because it effectively denied a federal right. The Supreme Court might plausibly have ruled that federal law had to govern the procedure for raising federal rights in state courts. However, just as a state court enforcing the law of another state generally may follow its own procedures, the Supreme Court ordinarily[186] allows state law to govern raising federal issues in state courts in order to honor the state's interest in an orderly judicial system.

Justice Brennan cut to the essence of the problem in *Henry*: a state procedural ground may preclude consideration of a federal right only if "the State's insistence on compliance with its procedural rule serves a legitimate state interest. In every case we must inquire whether the enforcement of a procedural forfeiture serves such a state interest." Otherwise, he implied, applying the state rule would offend the Supremacy Clause by unreasonably interfering with enforcing of federal law.

Unfortunately, the very next sentence acknowledged that, "[t]he Mississippi rule requiring contemporaneous objection to the introduction of illegal evidence clearly does serve a legitimate state interest," and elaborated on the point. One might expect

---

[186] The exceptions are if state law discriminates against federal law or is unconstitutional.

the opinion to have ended there with an affirmance, but the Court went on to say, having just recited why contemporaneous objection is important, that Henry's motions for directed verdict "may have substantially served" the state's interest. The Court did *not* say that Mississippi's procedural rule was unconstitutional as applied. It simply declined to treat the default as an adequate and independent state ground. Note that some of Justice Brennan's language appears to be an evaluation of the contemporaneous-objection on its face. But other language was at least ambiguous as to whether the test of the state rule was an on-its-face or an as-applied test.

Justice Brennan's application left something to be desired. Applying the Mississippi rule, he suggested, served no legitimate interest in *Henry.* Henry's motions for a directed verdict at the close of the state's case and when the defendant rested enabled the judge to redress the wrong by hearing more argument on search-and-seizure and, if necessary, instructing the jury to disregard the evidence.[187]

The Court's opinion may raise more questions than it answers. Obviously Mississippi did not

---

[187] It is hard to believe he really had much confidence in a jury's ability to ignore incriminating testimony whose reliability was not in question; the Court could have avoided prejudice to the defendant only by ordering a new trial.

think that a directed verdict motion after admission of the questionable evidence was sufficient; else it would not have had and enforced the contemporaneous-objection rule. Yet the Court did not say that the rule was unconstitutional as applied. It is reasonable to wonder about the legitimacy of the Court's suggestion that the rule should not apply. If the state rule is constitutional, why should the state have to settle for "substantially served"? A contemporaneous-objection rule is not so unusual that the court should excuse even out-of-state counsel (Henry had both local and out-of-state counsel) from complying with it.[188]

Henry did not actually decide whether the state ground was adequate. It remanded for a determination whether the failure to object contemporaneously had been deliberate. If a litigant chooses not to take advantage of the opportunity to raise an issue in the trial court, the Court seemed to be saying, he should not be permitted to raise it on appeal. In doing so, the Court harked back to habeas corpus cases reluctant to find waiver of constitutional rights unless there was a "deliberate bypass" of "the

---

[188] Besides, as you may recall if you saw MY COUSIN VINNY (Twentieth Century Fox, 1992), counsel appearing in any court, even *pro haec vice*, must know and follow the court's procedural rules.

orderly procedure of the state courts * * * ."[189] Today it is clear that procedural default in the state
courts very likely will prevent Supreme Court review unless counsel can establish that the state
rule is at least unconstitutional as applied.

Suppose a party does violate a state procedural
rule about raising an issue, but the highest state
court that can hear the case considers and rules upon it anyway. The earlier procedural default does
not prevent Supreme Court review. If the state
court elects not to regard the rule violation as pre-
venting its consideration of the issue, the Supreme
Court can review the decision that the state court
made, even if the state court would have been justified in refusing to consider the issue under the almost universal use-it-or-lose-it rule.

4. Finality

Section 1257's grant of jurisdiction to the Court
to review "[f]inal judgments or decrees * * *" has
acquired an oxymoronic quality because the Court
has now defined four categories of state judgments
eligible for review even though there are further
proceedings to come in the state courts.   In 1945,
Court acknowledged an accumulation of circumstances that saw "a departure from this require-

---

[189] The Court has since rejected the deliberate-bypass standard
in habeas cases. *See infra* notes 207-213 and accompanying text.

ment of finality for federal jurisdiction."[190]   The
Court has attempted justify the departure as the
"best way" to avoid needless litigation and wasting
time.   (At least the Court has insisted that there
have been a final determination of the federal issue
by the state courts and that there not be other federal issues that might require later review.)

A later case[191] set out the categories.   Category
1 includes "cases in which there are further proceedings—even entire trials—yet to occur in the
state courts but where for one reason or another the
federal issue is conclusive or the outcome of further
proceedings preordained," the latter occurring if the
party seeking review acknowledges that its only
possibility of prevailing is on the federal question.
Category 2 includes "cases * * * in which the federal
issue, finally decided by the highest court in the
State, will survive and require decision regardless
of the outcome of future state-court proceedings."
One might regard both categories as the Court saying to the litigants, "Well, you can see us now or see
us later."   However, the Court spoke before Congress eliminated virtually all review by appeal in

---

[190] Radio Station WOW, Inc. v. Johnson, 326 U.S. 120, 124
(1945).   The potential separation-of-powers problems with the
Court deciding to depart from an explicit statutory criterion are
too obvious for discussion, particularly because Congress *did*
provide some interlocutory appeals from the district to the circuit courts.   But no Congress has altered the Court's course.

[191] Cox Broadcasting Corp. v. Cohn, 420 U.S. 469 (1975).

favor of certiorari, so the inevitability of the case arriving at the Court has faded.

Category 3 holds cases "where the federal claim has been finally decided, with further proceedings on the merits in the state courts to come, but in which later review of the federal issue cannot be had, whatever the ultimate outcome of the case." Thus, for example, if the state's highest court has found a Fourth Amendment violation and remanded for a new trial, the Fourth-Amendment issue cannot survive for Supreme Court review. Whether the defendant is acquitted or convicted in the second trial, the exclusion of the evidence takes the Fourth-Amendment issue out of the case. So if one conceptualizes the first two categories as the Court's now-or-later formulation, then Category 3 is the now-or-never formulation.

Category 4, as Justice Rehnquist's dissent suggested, is not susceptible to paraphrasing.

> Lastly, there are those situations where the federal issue has been finally decided in the state courts with further proceedings pending in which the party seeking review here might prevail on the merits on nonfederal grounds, thus rendering unnecessary review of the federal issue by this Court, and where reversal of the state court on the federal issue would be preclusive of any further litigation on

the relevant cause of action rather than merely controlling the nature and character of, or determining the admissibility of evidence in, the state proceedings still to come. In these circumstances, if a refusal immediately to review the state court decision might seriously erode federal policy, the Court has entertained and decided the federal issue, which itself has been finally determined by the state courts for purposes of the state litigation.

The Court described this variation on "finality" as "consistent with the pragmatic approach that we have followed in the past in determining finality." This seems to be the Court's a-bird-in-the-hand-is-worth-two-in-the-bush approach. Perhaps it is, but the Court's eagerness to reach federal—often constitutional issues—that it might otherwise never have to adjudicate to resolve the dispute flies in the face of its oft-repeated commitment to avoiding needless decision of constitutional issues.

The bottom line is that the Court has authorized four sets of appeals that look like interlocutory appeals, despite Congress's restriction of the Court's jurisdiction to "[f]inal judgments or decrees." One might try to put a salutary gloss on the practice by arguing that in all four categories, at least the decision of the federal issue is final. The only problem is the Court's own long-standing view that, "This Court, however, reviews judgments, not statements in opinions."[192]

The categories' existence also poses an unanswerable question for counsel. Suppose a case that arguably fits in one of the categories—especially Category 4, since it is so amorphous. The highest state court has made a final decision on a federal issue, but there are further state-court proceedings to come. What is counsel to do? Generally, counsel has only ninety days to file a petition for certiorari.[193] But ninety days from when? If counsel waits for all state proceedings to end before filing, the petition may be untimely if the interlocutory decision qualified for immediate appeal. On the other hand, if counsel follows the most conservative course and files for certiorari within ninety days of the interlocutory decision, the Supreme Court will have many more petitions to dispose of, and the litigants will be simultaneously seeking Supreme Court review and engaging in the further state-court proceedings (unless there is a stay). What would you do to protect your client?

C. Appellate Review of Federal Decisions

Section 1254 governs appeals from the circuit courts. Subject-matter jurisdiction is less of a prob-

---

[192] McClung v. Silliman, 19 U.S. (6 Wheat.) 598 (1821).

[193] 28 U.S.C. § 2101(c).

lem in this area, since the lower courts should have resolved it. That section now dispenses with the finality requirement from the very beginning, noting specifically that review by certiorari is possible "before or after rendition of judgment or decree." There is, however, a finality requirement in 28 U.S.C. § 1291, which governs appeals from the district courts to the courts of appeals.

The Court took liberties with the finality requirement under § 1291 as it has under § 1257.[194] More recently, the Court has been reluctant to extend these precedents to other interlocutory rulings. *United States v. MacDonald*[195] refused to allow an appeal from the denial of a pretrial motion to dismiss for failure to afford a speedy trial, distinguishing *Abney* on the ground that the Double Jeopardy Clause gave a right not to be tried at all that could not be vindicated by later review. Similarly, *Coopers & Lybrand v. Livesay*[196] rejected the so-called "death knell" doctrine, which had allowed immediate appeal from the refusal to certify a class action when the plaintiffs personal stake was so small

---

[194] *E.g.*, Abney v. United States, 431 U.S. 651 (1977) (holding "final" the denial of a motion to dismiss on double-jeopardy grounds); Cohen v. Beneficial Indus. Loan Corp., 337 U.S. 541 (1949) (reviewing the applicability of a state law that required the plaintiff in a shareholder's action to post security for costs).

[195] 435 U.S. 850 (1978).

[196] 437 U.S. 463 (1978).

that he was unlikely to continue the suit individually. The principle of irreparable harm, which underlay both *Abney* and *Cohen*, seemed applicable to *Coopers* as well; yet the Court emphasized that loose construction of finality would undermine congressional limitations on interlocutory review in § 1292(b).

The Court seems to construe the finality requirement more strictly in reviewing federal than state determinations. One might have expected the opposite, both because of federalism concerns and because of the difference in language: Justice Frankfurter once suggested that a final "decision" under § 1291 is not the same as a final "judgment" under § 1257. On the other hand, interlocutory appealability under § 1291 means interruption of an ongoing trial-court proceeding; under § 1257 the question is usually whether to review a state appellate decision after completion of trial proceedings.

D. Post-Conviction Review

1. Federal Habeas Corpus

a. The Issues Cognizable

In recent decades, most judicial review of state criminal convictions for constitutional error has come through habeas corpus in the district courts instead of by appeal or petition for certiorari in the Supreme Court under § 1257. The law governing this collateral review of state-court judgments is absurdly complex and tends to change with every membership change on the Court. At the outset, note that the writ of habeas corpus merely commands the custodian to bring the detained individual before the court so that the court can examine the detention's legality. When a court grants *the writ*, it merely launches the judicial inquiry. Whether the court subsequently grants relief under the writ is a separate question.

The basic statutory provision regarding habeas corpus is 28 U.S.C. § 2241, which makes the writ available to any person who is "in custody in violation of the Constitution or laws or treaties of the United States." This never has meant that everyone whose conviction is tainted by an error of federal law is entitled to relief. Until recently there were stringent limitations on the kinds of federal issues petitioners could raise on habeas corpus in attacking a criminal conviction. Habeas was initially a device for testing the validity of executive detention; ordinary principles of finality precluded collateral attack on any judgment rendered by a competent court. Thus habeas could challenge a conviction only for lack of jurisdiction. On at least two early occasions, however, the Court allowed habeas review of questions that were not jurisdictional—double jeopardy and the constitutionality of the statute under which the petitioner had been convicted. But these decisions seem to have been exceptions to the general rule that habeas could not function as an appeal, a rule stemming from the fact that jurisdictional statutes for the district courts confer only original jurisdiction, and those for the circuit courts permit appeals only from the district courts.[197]

Later cases greatly extended the issues habeas corpus could address. *Johnson v. Zerbst*,[198] while adhering to the formula that only jurisdictional questions could be raised, concluded that denial of counsel was so fundamental that it undermined jurisdiction. *Waley v. Johnston*[199] abandoned the fiction of jurisdiction altogether, permitting a petitioner to question whether his guilty plea was coerced because he could not effectively have raised the issue in the original proceeding.

Brown v. Allen[200] went still further, determining the voluntariness of a confession although the state court had already heard and decided the issue. *Fay v. Noia*,[201] held that any federal constitu-

---

[197] Since 1923 the Court has emphasized that the inferior federal courts cannot hear cases (no matter how styled) that effectively appeal from state-court judgments, a doctrine known as the *Rooker-Feldman* doctrine. *See* Chapter VI. *Rooker-Feldman* does not apply to habeas because of Congress's specific grant of district court jurisdiction in § 2241.

[198] 304 U.S. 458 (1938).

[199] 316 U.S. 101 (1942).

[200] 344 U.S. 443 (1953).

[201] 372 U.S. 391 (1963), *overruled by* Coleman v. Thompson, 501 U.S. 722 (1991).

tional question was open on habeas corpus, and *Kaufman v. United States*[202] seemed to say the same was true for a federal prisoner seeking relief under 28 U.S.C. § 2255. Nevertheless, the federal courts will not consider every allegation of constitutional error on its merits in a habeas proceeding.

The Court and the Anti-Terrorism and Effective Death Penalty Act (AEDPA) have narrowed the issues habeas can address, largely by limiting decisions' retroactivity. *Teague v. Lane*[203] announced that, in almost every circumstance, new constitutional rules that the Court announces in habeas cases should not apply retroactively, unless (1) the new rule exempts certain individual conduct from the criminal law, or (2) the new rule concerns procedures "implicit in the concept of ordered liberty." AEDPA picked up the baton from *Teague*, specifying in § 2254(d) that habeas relief for state prisoners is appropriate only if the state's adjudication was either (1) contrary to or an unreasonable application of "clearly established Federal law, as determined by the Supreme Court," or (2) rested on an "unreasonable determination of the facts."

Williams (Terry) v. Taylor,[204] although the Court was fractured, made clear that a mere error

---

[202] 394 U.S. 217 (1969).

[203] 489 U.S. 288 (1989).

[204] 539 U.S. 362 (2000).

of federal law is insufficient to meet the first prong—a state court's interpretation of federal law may be wrong without being unreasonable. Justice Stevens disagreed on that point, but did agree that a state court's decision of whether a rule was "new" for § 2254(d) purposes could indeed be wrong without being unreasonable. (Query, though, how clearly established the law that the Court had announced could have been if the state court could be wrong without being unreasonable.)

The rationale is that, almost without exception, federal courts reviewing state criminal convictions should review them under the law that existed at the time of the state adjudication. New rules that the Court announces in direct-review cases get retroactive effect to the extent that the Court's general approach to retroactivity permits—in all cases on still pending on direct review when the Court announces the new rule.

b. The Impact of a Prior State-Court Decision

Brown v. Allen, challenging a state court's rejection of a coerced-confession claim, also raised the issue of res judicata. Even if the confession question was within the federal court's habeas jurisdiction, why wasn't the state-court determination of that question binding? The Full-Faith-and-Credit

Act[205] appears to require it: "the same full faith and credit * * * as they have * * * in the courts * * * from which they are taken." Without mentioning the statute, *Brown* held res judicata inapplicable in habeas cases, a result subsequent cases and statutes have partially overturned.

Nevertheless the conclusion was correct. Section 2254(b) then in force precluded relief "unless * * * the applicant has exhausted the remedies available in the courts of the State." The clear implication was that federal relief was available after state courts had adjudicated the petitioner's claims. Thus, original § 2254(b) created an exception to § 1738 and to the ordinary principles of res judicata.

It followed that a federal court could reexamine *de novo* questions of law and of ultimate fact—such as whether, if the defendant had been beaten by the police, his confession was involuntary. On basic fact issues, however—such as whether the defendant had been beaten—a state-court finding was preclusive absent a "vital flaw" in the state proceedings. *Townsend v. Sain*[206] modified this standard, holding that the federal court should reexamine even basic fact-finding unless the state court had afforded the defendant a "full and fair" hearing.

---

[205] 28 U.S.C. § 1738.

[206] 372 U.S. 293 (1963), *overruled*, Keeney v. Tamayo Reyes, 504 U.S. 1 (1992).

But *Keeney v. Tamayo-Reyes*[207] overruled *Townsend*, rejecting the *Fay-v.-Noia* deliberate-bypass standard. *Keeney* required that to get a federal evidentiary hearing, a habeas petitioner who failed adequately to develop the factual record in state court proceedings had to show cause and prejudice.

AEDPA[208] reduced federal habeas corpus challenges to state court convictions even more. Section 2254(d) now precludes reexamination of "any claim that was adjudicated on the merits in State court proceedings" unless the adjudication resulted in a decision that was (1) "contrary to, or involved an unreasonable application of, clearly established Federal law, as determined by the Supreme Court of the United States" or (2) "based on an unreasonable determination of the facts in light of the evidence presented in the State court proceedings." This provision limits redetermination of questions of law as well as fact. Section 2254(e) further limits the federal court's ability to take new evidence.

Stone v. Powell[209] held that state-court adjudication of a Fourth-Amendment claim precludes habeas relief. Petitioners argued that the prosecution used evidence obtained in violation of the Fourth Amendment. In language reminiscent of *Townsend*

---

[207] 504 U.S. 1 (1992).

[208] Pub. L. No. 104-132, 110 Stat. 1214 (1996).

[209] 428 U.S. 465 (1976).

v. Sain, the Court held that habeas was unavailable because the state courts had afforded the prisoners "an opportunity for full and fair litigation." The exclusionary rule existed not to improve the truth-finding process but to deter wrongdoing by the police. The Court found the marginal deterrence provided by a second opportunity to litigate the search's legality did not justify the cost of reopening the proceeding.

Stone emphasized that it was not holding the court without jurisdiction or laying down general principles to govern habeas litigation; it was clarifying the scope of the exclusionary rule. *Stone* is inapplicable to other issues. For example, *Jackson v. Virginia*[210] held that a full and fair state hearing did not preclude considering whether there was constitutionally adequate evidence to sustain a guilty verdict, because the issue was "central to the basic question of guilt or innocence." *Rose v. Mitchell*[211] held *Stone* inapplicable to a claim of discrimination in grand-jury selection. There was greater need for a federal forum because the state courts were reviewing alleged judicial (not executive) violations, and there was less invasion of state interests because the state could retry the defendant on the same evidence.

---

[210] 443 U.S. 307 (1979).
[211] 443 U.S. 545 (1979).

What constitutes "an opportunity for full and fair litigation" under *Stone* remains unclear. Nine circuits have said that a state court's error in Fourth-Amendment analysis is not denial of a full and fair opportunity. A few courts have said that a willful refusal by the state court to apply Fourth-Amendment law is a denial, but the petitioner's burden is a very heavy one. Providing an opportunity to litigate the issue in the state system is what counts; a defendant's failure to invoke the procedure precludes habeas relief.

c. Procedural Defaults

Habeas petitioners may also be ineligible for federal relief for failing properly to raise a federal claim in the state court. Res judicata originally did not apply in habeas proceedings, but a modified form of the doctrine now does apply, first recognized by the Court and then enacted in AEDPA at 28 U.S.C. § 2254(d). *Fay v. Noia* had declared that the petitioner's failure to follow state procedural rules in attempting to exhaust state remedies barred habeas review only if the petitioner deliberately bypassed state procedures. A state *judgment* was immune from Supreme Court review if supported by an adequate state ground. At that time, the Court deemed habeas a challenge to *custody*, not to the underlying judgment. No judgment was necessary to support a habeas petition. That effectively meant that the adequate-and-independent-state-ground doctrine did not apply to procedural questions on habeas corpus. But in *Noia*, the adequate-and-independent-state-ground doctrine should have applied for the same reasons it applies on direct review. To decide the federal question alone would run afoul of the prohibition on advisory opinions cases; to decide the state-law question would be beyond the Court's jurisdiction under *Murdock v. Memphis*.

But to say the adequate-state-ground doctrine should have applied is not to say that the state ground was adequate. *Henry v. Mississippi*[212] (an appeal of a criminal conviction rather than a habeas case) seemed to rule that the relevant question is whether applying the state procedural rule imposes an unreasonable burden on enforcing a federal right. The Court appeared to commit federal courts hearing habeas petitions from state prisoners to evaluating state procedural defaults on a case-by-case basis, using an indefinite standard of "whether enforcement of the rule *here*" (emphasis added) would serve a substantial interest or "would be to force resort to an arid ritual of meaningless form."

In *Wainwright v. Sykes*,[213] however, the Court cited *Henry* but omitted the individualized analysis that *Henry* seemed to prescribe. *Sykes* also aban-

---

[212] The discussion of *Henry* appears *supra* at 127.

[213] 433 U.S. 72 (1977).

doned *Noia*'s lenient approach toward state procedural defaults. Sykes argued that he had not received adequate warnings under *Miranda v Arizona*[214] before making incriminating statements. He had not objected to introduction of those statements at trial, as state law required, and the Court held that was fatal to his petition.

The Court invoked neither exhaustion nor waiver, nor did it bother to refute *Noia*'s argument against applying the adequate-state-ground doctrine. An adequate state ground would preclude review "in the federal courts," and the state-law ground in *Sykes* would barred direct Supreme Court review. But it stopped short of saying the adequacy of the state ground barred habeas corpus also; instead it relied upon what it described as "the rule" of in *Davis v. United States*.[215]

Davis had been in federal prison, and he could not challenge the makeup of his grand jury for the first time in a post-conviction motion because Rule 12(b)(2) of the Federal Rules of Criminal Procedure required such an objection before trial. *Francis v. Henderson*[216] took the next step, applying the same requirement to a state prisoner because "there is no reason to * * * give greater preclusive effect to pro-

---

[214] 384 U.S. 486 (1966).

[215] 411 U.S. 333 (1974).

[216] 425 U.S. 536 (1976).

cedural defaults by federal defendants than to similar defaults by state defendants."[217] *Francis* (and *Sykes*, extending *Francis* to *Miranda* objections) created a judge-made doctrine of forfeiture in deference to state interests. In both cases, the Court added that the default rule would not bar habeas if the prisoner made "a showing of cause for the non-compliance and * * * actual prejudice resulting from the alleged constitutional violation," as Rule 12(b) required.

These decisions established the adequate-state-ground doctrine in habeas-corpus proceedings attacking state convictions. *Coleman v. Thompson*[218] committed the Court to that position explicitly, the majority opinion specifying that it did so as a matter of comity and federalism. On direct review (at least with respect to substantive state grounds), the Court had declared that proceeding in the face of an adequate and independent state ground would cause the Court to render advisory opinions, violating the Case-or-Controversy Clause.

The Court now requires a habeas petitioner to show cause and prejudice underlying the procedural default. What constitutes sufficient "cause"?

---

[217] There was one very good reason for such a distinction: Federal Rule 12 was binding on the federal court, while the parallel state rule was not.

[218] 501 U.S. 722 (1991).

Simple attorney error does not; incompetence of counsel in the constitutional sense would, though the defendant must first present the ineffective-assistance claim to the state courts. Failure to raise a claim is also excusable if the claim is "so novel that its legal basis is not reasonably available to counsel," or if the state has concealed the evidence on which the claim rests. Yet while the novelty of the claim may justify failure to raise it in the original proceeding, it may defeat habeas on another ground; *Teague v. Lane*[219] sharply cut back on retroactive application of new criminal procedure rules in habeas proceedings, and 28 U.S.C. § 2254(d) limited it even further, recognizing only Supreme Court cases as applicable precedent—lest guilty persons become entitled to a new trial after evidence has disappeared.

With respect to prejudice, the petitioner has a heavy burden. If he complains of jury instructions, he must show that the instructions were so bad that the conviction is tainted.[220] For other challenges to convictions, (most frequently "actual innocence" by reason of new evidence), the Court's approach before AEDPA required the petitioner to show by a preponderance of the evidence that no reasonable juror would have convicted if the new

---

[219] 489 U.S. 288 (1989).

[220] United States v. Frady, 456 U.S. 152 (1982).

evidence had been available.[221] However, AEDPA requires a greater showing: (1) in-ability to discover the underlying facts earlier through due diligence, and (2) "the facts underlying the claim, if proven and viewed in light of the evidence as a whole, would be sufficient to establish by clear and convincing evidence that, but for constitutional error, no reasonable factfinder would have found the applicant guilty of the underlying offense." Thus, AEDPA increases the petitioner's burden from preponderance to clear and convincing evidence.

d. Federal Prisoners

Habeas corpus lies for federal as well as state prisoners. Originally, prisoners originally had to seek habeas relief in the district where they were confined (because habeas is a remedy addressed to custody, not conviction). In 1948, Congress enacted 28 U.S.C. § 2255, a new post-conviction remedy available in the district of trial. Congress intended the remedy to be as broad as habeas but to relieve inordinate caseloads on the courts in districts with federal prisons and entrust the task to a court already familiar with the case.

Kaufman v. United States held § 2255 available for search-and-seizure claims, and *Davis v. United States* held it applicable to the nonconstitutional

---

[221] Shlup v. Delo, 513 U.S. 298 (1995).

claim that the regulation supporting conviction was invalid owing to a supervening change in the law. But dictum in *Davis* and *United States v. Timmreck*[222] reaffirmed that § 2255 is available only to correct non-constitutional defects that are "fundamental." That Davis had arguably committed no crime was fundamental; that the sentencing court omitted to advise Timmreck only of the mandatory parole period following his release from custody was not. The same standard applies to non-constitutional habeas claims from state prisoners.

Sanders v. United States[223] remains the last important decision on the effect of prior proceedings in a § 2255 case. As in habeas for state prisoners at the time, the Court held res judicata inapplicable but declared that a federal prisoner could not relitigate an issue that had full and fair consideration on an earlier § 2255 motion. Under *Sanders*, even questions of law, which for a state prisoner rated *de novo* review, were immune from reexamination absent "intervening change in the law" or other extraordinary circumstances.

Sanders could have rested on § 2255's provision that the court "shall not be required to entertain a second or successive motion for similar relief on behalf of the same prisoner." But it did not, and in

---

[222] 441 U.S. 780 (1979).
[223] 373 U.S. 1 (1963).

dictum, *Kaufman* suggested that *Sanders* might apply to an adjudication in the trial. Section 2255 clearly disfavors second or successive petitions, requiring either

> (1) newly discovered evidence that, if proven and viewed in light of the evidence as a whole, would be sufficient to establish by clear and convincing evidence that no reasonable factfinder would have found the movant guilty of the offense; or

> (2) a new rule of constitutional law, made retroactive to cases on collateral review by the Supreme Court, that was previously unavailable.

Specific provisions of the Federal Rules of Criminal Procedure may impose even more stringent forfeiture requirements, and subsequent restrictions on habeas for state prisoners suggest that the Court will be less receptive to the claims of federal prisoners as well.

e. Military Prisoners

As if all this were not complicated enough, yet another body of law governs post-conviction relief for military prisoners. Originally, habeas could challenge only the jurisdiction of the military court, reflecting the then-existing limitation on nonmilitary habeas relief. There was no suggestion that review was narrower in military than in other cases.

   Burns v. Wilson[224] is still the leading case. There was no majority opinion, and only Justice Minton adhered to the old jurisdiction rule. Speaking for a plurality, Chief Justice Vinson stated the test in a form that lower courts have often repeated: the question is whether the military tribunal afforded a "full and fair hearing" on federal constitutional claims. A similar test had applied to civil prisoners before *Brown v. Allen*, but five Justices made clear they thought habeas narrower for military than for civil prisoners.

   Since *Burns*, the Court has spoken only obliquely on military post-conviction review. *United States v. Augenblick*,[225] was a civil suit for back pay, attacking a discharge based upon a court-martial. The first obstacle was 10 U.S.C. § 876, which makes military criminal proceedings "final and conclusive" and "binding" on the federal courts, but the statute did not bar habeas corpus because of the Suspension Clause.[226] Committee reports expressly recognized the habeas exception when Congress recodified the finality provision. In *Augenblick*, the Court of Claims said § 876 did not bar back-pay suits ei-

---

[224] 346 U.S. 137 (1953).

[225] 393 U.S. 348 (1969).

[226] U.S. CONST. art. I, § 9, cl. 2.

ther, but the Supreme Court held that the issues raised—the necessity for corroboration and the right to examine witness statements—were not cognizable because not of constitutional dimension. The Court did not say whether the same limitation would apply to military habeas.

Schlesinger v. Councilman[227] added useful dicta on military post-conviction review, refusing an injunction against a pending court-martial because the plaintiff had failed to exhaust military remedies. The Court said the finality clause of § 876 merely embodied normal principles of res judicata, which allowed not only habeas but other post-conviction remedies as well for "lack of jurisdiction or some other equally fundamental defect." But, "[g]rounds of impeachment cognizable in habeas proceedings may not be sufficient to warrant other forms of collateral relief," for whether petitioner may raise the issue may turn in part upon "the gravity of the harm from which relief is sought." The Court allowed the military prosecution of Councilman for an off-post sale and gift of marijuana to go forward, relying on the abstention principles of *Younger v. Harris*.

Given the lack of guidance, lower courts have split on the scope of post-conviction review of military tribunals. Several courts of appeals continue

---

[227] 420 U.S. 738 (1975).

to adhere to *Burns v. Wilson*. Others, however, allow a broader review. *Calley v. Calloway*[228] prescribed a four-part test: (1) the issue must be jurisdictional, constitutional, or "fundamental" in the sense of *Davis v. United States*; (2) the court will defer to military findings on questions of fact if there has been a "full and fair" hearing; (3) the court will resolve questions of law *de novo*; (4) the court will give considerable deference to military findings that discipline requires different substantive rules.

The lower courts also are in disarray about the effect of procedural defaults in military proceedings on the availability of habeas corpus. Some have said if petitioner never raised the issue, the military did not afford a full and fair hearing, making the issue reviewable. Others courts have disagreed. The Fifth Circuit once said *Fay v. Noia* applied to military proceedings. *Wainwright v. Sykes* requires reexamination of this question.

The scope of post-conviction review for those convicted of military offenses remains largely a mystery. The military prisoner—like his state-criminal counterpart and unlike the federal prisoner—may never have had an opportunity to present his federal arguments to an Article III court. But broad habeas for military convicts would arguably

---

[228] 519 F.2d 184 (5th Cir. 1075).

have been inconsistent with the policy of military independence that appeared to underlie Congress's consistent refusal to provide direct civilian review of military convictions. Congress's decision to permit Supreme Court review of certain decisions of the Court of Appeals for the Armed Forces (28 U.S.C. § 1259) puts this question in a different light.

f. Custody, Venue, and Prematurity

(1) Custody

Habeas corpus is not available to everyone who has been unconstitutionally convicted; under § 2241, the writ is only for a person in "custody." Someone who has received only a fine cannot use habeas corpus. But it is not necessary that the petitioner be in jail; habeas is the appropriate vehicle to test an allegedly unlawful induction into the military and to determine which parent is entitled to child custody.

Jones v. Cunningham[229] held that a convict on parole was in sufficient "custody" to support habeas corpus because he was subject to significant restraints on his liberty that the public generally did not share. He was not allowed to leave town, to move from one home to another, or to drive a car without the consent of his parole officer. The Court relied on cases holding that habeas lay to test the

---

[229] 371 U.S. 236 (1963).

right of aliens to enter the country even though they were "free to go anywhere else in the world." Finally, *Carafas v. LaVallee* held that when the petitioner had been in custody when he filed for habeas corpus, though released before decision, he was entitled to the writ. The custody requirement applies only at filing, and the case was not moot because it involved a felony conviction with collateral consequences after imprisonment ended.

Hensley v. Municipal Court[230] watered the custody requirement down almost beyond recognition in holding that a petitioner was "in custody" while released on his own recognizance pending review of a jail sentence. The dissenters protested that the sole restraint on Hensley was the duty to appear in court when called; he was "under no greater restriction than one who had been subpoenaed to testify." The Court was concerned about the arbitrariness of an interpretation that would have required the petitioner to spend ten minutes in jail in order to obtain habeas review.

One may also be held unconstitutionally although not entitled to unrestricted freedom. *In re Bonner*[231] held that habeas lay when the petitioner had been locked up in the wrong jail. The lower courts were slow to follow *Bonner*'s implications

---

[230] 411 U.S. 345 (1973).

[231] 151 U.S. 242 (1894).

with respect to unconstitutional prison conditions, but the Court gave such claims a boost by its remark in *Wilwording v. Swenson*[232] that allegations of inadequate prison facilities and physical mistreatment were "cognizable on federal habeas corpus" as well as under the civil-rights statute. The Prison Litigation Reform Act of 1995 now requires exhaustion of "all available" administrative remedies as a prerequisite to habeas relief.

(2) Venue

In *Braden v. 30th Judicial Circuit Court*,[233] petitioner was in an Alabama prison but attacked Kentucky's failure to grant him a speedy trial on a Kentucky offense. Section 2241 authorizes federal judges to issue habeas "within their respective jurisdictions," and an earlier decision had construed that to require filing in the district of custody. Nevertheless, observing that Kentucky was a more appropriate place to try a case concerning a Kentucky offense, the Supreme Court upheld the power of the Kentucky district court to hear the petition: § 2241 required no "more than that the court issuing the writ have jurisdiction over the custodian." Practicality prevailed over the language of a poorly drafted statute.

---

[232] 404 U.S. 249 (1971).

[233] 410 U.S. 484 (1973).

(3) Prematurity

Prematurity was originally a serious obstacle to a petitioner seeking to challenge one of two or more consecutive sentences by habeas corpus. A petitioner could not challenge a future sentence while serving a valid sentence, because he was then not unlawfully in custody. Lower courts had held that the first sentence could not be attacked while it was being served either, because even if they set it set aside, the prisoner would still be lawfully in custody under the unchallenged second sentence. *Walker v. Wainwright*[234] disapproved the latter position and *Peyton v. Rowe*[235] the former, stretching the language of § 2241 in recognition of the desirability of reviewing convictions while evidence was still available and before the prisoner began doing time he was arguably entitled not to serve.

Whether *Walker* and *Rowe* apply to federal prisoners seeking relief under § 2255 is not clear, for in addition to requiring that the applicant be in federal custody that section limits the writ to persons "claiming the right to be released." The Fourth Circuit mentioned in dictum that a case like *Rowe* would satisfy the requirement because the petitioner sought release "from all of the burdens of the invalid sentence." A better argument might be

---

[234] 390 U.S. 335 (1968).

[235] 391 U.S. 54 (1968).

that Congress intended § 2255 intended to be as broad as habeas, and the statute further provides that if the remedy it provides is insufficient, habeas will lie.

g. Successive Petitions

First the Court[236] and then AEDPA[237] disapproved successive petitions. The Court required the petitioner to show cause and prejudice for failing to raise the issue in the original petition. AEDPA now requires that the petitioner secure a certificate permitting the district court to hear the successive petition from a panel of the circuit court. The panel's decision is not reviewable, by either a petition for rehearing or a petition for certiorari. AEDPA instructs the circuit court to dismiss, unless—

> (A) the applicant shows that the claim relies on a new rule of constitutional law, made retroactive to cases on collateral review by the Supreme Court, that was previously unavailable; or
>
> (B) (i) the factual predicate for the claim could not have been discovered previously through the exercise of due diligence; and

---

[236] McCleskey v. Zant, 499 U.S. 467 (1991).

[237] 28 U.S.C. § 2244(b)(3)(A).

(ii) the facts underlying the claim, if proven and viewed in light of the evidence as a whole, would be sufficient to establish by clear and convincing evidence that, but for constitutional error, no reasonable factfinder would have found the applicant guilty of the underlying offense.

2. Exhaustion of State Remedies

Notwithstanding the flat statutory command that habeas corpus lay on behalf of all persons "restrained of * * * liberty" in violation of federal law, *Ex parte Royall*[238] refused to allow a federal court to issue a writ that would have interfered with a pending state criminal proceeding, anticipating *Younger* abstention. To avoid "unnecessary conflict" between state and federal courts, a litigant must exhaust state-court remedies before seeking federal relief. The Court subsequently extended this requirement to final convictions, and Congress codified this aspect of the doctrine: a federal court may not grant a writ to "a person in custody pursuant to the judgment of a State court" unless (1) he has "exhausted the remedies available in the courts of

---

[238] 117 U.S. 241 (1886).

the State," (2) there is no corrective state process, or (3) the state process that does exist is ineffective.[239]

The exhaustion requirement is thus not absolute, even where it applies. A petitioner need not make repeated applications raising the same issue to the state courts. The petitioner may show that exhaustion is ineffective if "the state's highest court has recently rendered an adverse decision in an identical case, and * * * there is no reason to believe that the state court will change its position."[240]

Section 2254(b) exists to afford state courts a final opportunity to re-examine state convictions. Read literally, the exhaustion requirement applies to every habeas petition filed by a state prisoner, whether or not he challenges his conviction. *Wilwording v. Swenson* rejected the literal interpretation, allowing a state prisoner to challenge the conditions of his confinement under 42 U.S.C. § 1983 without exhausting state remedies, echoing an earlier case concerning the Civil Rights Act's lack of exhaustion requirements that the Court reaffirmed some years after *Wilwording*. However, concerned lest litigants undermine the exhaustion requirement by employing § 1983 in "traditional" habeas corpus cases, *Preiser v. Rodriguez*[241] requires ex-

---

[239] 28 U.S.C. § 2254(b).

[240] *E.g.*, Layton v. Carson, 479 F.2d 1275 (5th Cir. 1973).

[241] 411 U.S. 475 (1973). On the other hand, the Second

haustion of state-court remedies before challenging the loss of good-time credits because the question affects the "duration of the confinement itself."

When someone seeks habeas relief before conviction, the courts are likely to insist not only that state courts first decide the question but also that the trial be over, for habeas is unnecessary if there is an acquittal. Once again, however, the exhaustion requirement is not absolute. *Braden v. 30th Judicial Circuit Court*, for example, allowed federal habeas to determine petitioner's right to speedy trial. Noting that the state courts had already rejected this claim, the Court said Braden was seeking not to litigate "a federal defense to a criminal charge" but to "demand enforcement of the * * * obligation to bring him promptly to trial." It concluded that his petition would not "forestall a state prosecution" but merely require the state to "provide him with a state court forum." Similarly, *Fain v. Duff*[242] entertained a pre-trial habeas petition based upon double jeopardy after an unsuccessful state-court appeal. To set a sentence aside after conviction would have been inadequate to protect the right, which guards against not only a second

---

Circuit has held the mere fact that exhaustion would require a petitioner to spend the weekend in jail while waiting for the state appellate court to meet insufficient to justify immediate federal intervention.

[242] 488 F.2d 218 (5th Cir. 1974).

punishment but also the "rigors and dangers" of the second trial.

3. Other Post-Conviction Remedies

The writ of error *coram nobis* under the All Writs Act, 28 U.S.C. § 1651, which empowers federal courts to issue writs "necessary or appropriate in aid of their respective jurisdictions," is a second collateral remedy for review of criminal convictions. *United States v. Morgan*[243] upheld using *coram nobis* to test a federal criminal conviction. Morgan was then in state custody, but he challenged an earlier federal judgment the state judge relied upon to enhance the sentence for his state crime. Morgan had to resort to *coram nobis* because traditional post-conviction remedies were unavailable. Because Morgan attacked his conviction, Rule 35 (correction of illegal sentences) did not apply. Neither did § 2255, for although he challenged a federal conviction, he was in state, not federal, custody. It was not clear that he could get federal habeas relief either, because he did not challenge his state conviction, and he was not in custody on the federal conviction.[244]

---

[243] 346 U.S. 502 (1954).

[244] The dissents argued that § 2255's post-conviction remedy was exclusive and that the writ was not ancillary to the exercise of jurisdiction, as § 1651 required, since the criminal proceeding was over.

In short, the field of post-conviction remedies is both complex and confused and calls out for comprehensive congressional reappraisal. The problem is also highly politicized, however, especially when it comes to review of state supreme courts by federal district judges. Do not hold your breath waiting for clarification.

VI. THE *ROOKER-FELDMAN* DOCTRINE

The idea underlying the *Rooker-Feldman* doctrine appeared briefly in the preceding chapter: the inferior federal courts have no jurisdiction to review of the judgments of state courts.[245] The Supreme Court has discussed the doctrine only three times, twice to establish it in its present form and once to warn against overbroad use. The problem has arisen largely because of counsel's resourcefulness invoking the original jurisdiction of the district courts by framing complaints so that they do not sound like they are seeking appellate review.

The first such case[246] was straightforward. Plaintiffs, having lost in Indiana's highest court, sought Supreme Court review, but their appeal "failed because the record did not disclose the presence of any question constituting a basis for such a review." Undeterred, they brought an action in the district court arguing that the Indiana Supreme Court's judgment violated the Impairment Clause.[247] The district court dismissed for want of

---

[245] The Court has finally discarded the fiction that federal habeas cases review only custody rather than the judgment underlying the custody, recognizing instead that habeas jurisdiction is a specific grant of review jurisdiction to the district courts. Exxon Mobil Corp. v. Saudi Basic Indus. Corp., 544 U.S. 280, 292 n.8 (2005).

[246] Rooker v. Fidelity Trust Co., 263 U.S. 413 (1923).

[247] U.S. CONST. art. I, § 10, cl. 1.

subject-matter jurisdiction; the Supreme Court affirmed.

The Court noted that Congress had given the district courts only original jurisdiction. If there was an impairment issue, plaintiffs should have raised it in the state court and pursued it through the state appellate process. Plaintiffs had raised it only on a petition for rehearing in the Indiana Supreme Court, which summarily denied rehearing. The United States Supreme Court recognized counsel's ploy for what it was—an attempt to have a federal district court overturn the judgment of a state court—and refused to permit federal intervention.

Sixty years later, the Court revisited the subject,[248] and the case was more complex. Two applicants for admission to the District of Columbia bar sought waivers from the District of Columbia Court of Appeals[249] of the requirement under Rule 46(I)(b)(3) that they have attended "an approved law school." In a *per curiam* order, the District of Columbia court refused the waivers, whereupon the

---

[248] District of Columbia Court of Appeals v. Feldman, 460 U.S. 462 (1983).

[249] That court is a "state" court (really an Article-I court), do not mistake it for the United States Court of Appeals for the District of Columbia Circuit.

applicants filed for relief in the United States District Court for the District of Columbia.

The case turned on whether the district court had subject-matter jurisdiction, which in turn depended on whether the *per curiam* order was "a judicial [as opposed to an administrative] act." The district court found that it was judicial and dismissed for lack of jurisdiction. The circuit court found that plaintiffs had properly raised legal arguments in the district court, characterizing their waiver requests as non-judicial in nature because there was no claim of *legal* right to the waiver (despite a long letter to the Chief Judge of the District of Columbia Court of Appeals from one of the applicants' counsel that included references to constitutional and antitrust[250] issues that "Mr. Feldman is prepared to pursue in the United States District Court if necessary").

The Supreme Court disagreed. It found the proceedings in the District of Columbia Court of Appeals "judicial in nature," distinguishing those proceedings from other situations in which the Court had declined to apply *Rooker*.

> The proceedings were not legislative, ministerial, or administrative. The District of Columbia Court of Appeals did

---

[250] The Circuit Court affirmed dismissal of those as "insubstantial."

not "loo[k] to the future and chang[e] existing conditions by making a new rule to be applied thereafter to all or some part of those subject to its power." Nor did it engage in rulemaking or specify "the requirements of eligibility or the course of study for applicants for admission to the bar * * *." Nor did the District of Columbia Court of Appeals simply engage in ministerial action. Instead, the proceedings before the District of Columbia Court of Appeals involved a "judicial inquiry" in which the court was called upon to investigate, declare, and enforce "liabilities as they [stood] on present or past facts and under laws supposed already to exist."

But the Court made a distinction the lower courts had not. Although it disallowed federal court review of the District of Columbia court's ruling on the waiver requests, it noted that "[t]o the extent that [plaintiffs] mounted a general challenge to the constitutionality of Rule 46(I)(b)(3), however, the District Court did have subject matter jurisdiction over their complaints." Evaluating the rule's constitutionality did "not require review of a judicial decision in a particular case. The District Court, therefore, has subject matter jurisdiction over these elements of the * * * complaints."

In 2005, the Court revisited *Rooker-Feldman*, complaining that lower courts had improperly expanded the doctrine. *Exxon Mobil Corporation v. Saudi Basic Industries Corporation* (SABIC) involved parallel litigation in the state and federal courts. As always with parallel litigation, it is useful to have a time line showing the sequence of the proceedings.

State litigation	Federal litigation
SABIC files a complaint seeking royalties	
	ExxonMobil files seeking damages under FSIA
ExxonMobil answers, including its federal claims as state counter-claims	
	SABIC moves for dismissal under FSIA
	District court denies the motion
	SABIC takes interlocutory appeal
Jury returns verdict for ExxonMobil	
SABIC appeals to Delaware Supreme Court	
	Third Circuit holds that entry of judgment in the state case required dismissal under *Rooker-Feldman*
	ExxonMobil obtains Supreme Court review by certiorari

SABIC began the state litigation, seeking royalties. Two weeks later, ExxonMobil began the federal action, alleging overcharging and invoking jurisdiction under the Foreign Sovereign Immunities Act of 1976 (FSIA). ExxonMobil then answered the state complaint, including as counterclaims the same causes of action it had alleged in the federal suit.

Before the state trial, the district court refused dismissal, finding jurisdiction under FISA. SABIC took an interlocutory appeal. Before the Third Circuit heard the appeal, the state-court jury returned a verdict for ExxonMobil, and, upon entry of judgment, SABIC appealed to the Delaware Supreme Court. While that appeal was pending, the Third Circuit ruled that the entry of judgment in the Delaware trial court required dismissal of the federal case under *Rooker-Feldman*. It reasoned that allowing the federal case to go to judgment potentially would invalidate the state court's judgment, something the Circuit thought flew in the face of *Rooker-Feldman*.

A unanimous Supreme Court reversed, based on the timing of the federal and state litigation: "The *Rooker–Feldman* doctrine * * * is confined to cases * * * brought by state-court losers complaining of injuries caused by state-court judgments rendered *before* the district court proceedings commenced and inviting district court review and rejection of those judgments." (Emphasis added.) That did not mean that a federal action in such circumstances should necessarily proceed; the district courts can stay federal actions or, in some circumstances, refrain from adjudication by invoking one of the abstention doctrines. But "[d]isposition of the federal action, once the state-court determination is complete, would be governed by preclusion law * * * ," which, the Court pointed out, was not jurisdictional. "In parallel litigation, a federal court may be bound to recognize the claim- and issue-preclusive effects of a state-court judgment, but federal jurisdiction over an action does not terminate automatically on the entry of judgment in the state court."

In any case with *Rooker-Feldman* potential, it still is necessary to do some careful analysis, along three axes: (1) the type of relief sought in the federal action, (2) whether the proper characterization of the federal action is "appeal," "collateral attack," or "independent action," and (3) whether there is standing.

A. Type of Relief

The basic distinction from *Feldman* continues. If a plaintiff challenges extant *rules* on federal grounds, the case may proceed, but if the challenge is to a *ruling* of a judicial body, it may not. Thus, when an attorney seeking reinstatement to a state bar attacked "various constitutional defects in the procedural rules" under which the state supreme court considered petitions for readmission, the action was proper.[251] The Third Circuit distinguished that case from one in which the relief the disbarred attorney sought to "force the district court to *review the merits* of the state court's decision * * * ," (emphasis added), the precise distinction upon which *Feldman* focused.[252] The attorney erred in the latter case by seeking an injunction against enforcement of the state supreme court's disbarment order on alleged constitutional grounds. The fact that the attorney had requested that the injunction apply to all future such cases involving attorneys did not transform his request from one seeking review of his individual case into a generalized attack on the rules underlying the decision.

B. Appeal, Collateral Attack, or Independent Action?

It is not always easy to characterize the federal action in situations that might call for applying *Rooker-Feldman*. When a dispute arose over whether a bank properly paid interest on real estate escrow accounts, an Alabama state court certi-

---

[251] Centifanti v. Nix, 865 F.2d 1422 (3d Cir. 1989).

[252] That distinction is perhaps somewhat counter-intuitive, because it makes the most broad-based challenges the ones most likely to have federal jurisdiction rather than the narrowest challenges.

fied a class that challenged the bank's actions.[253] The court subsequently approved a class settlement with attorneys' fees exceeding $8,000,000. The problem arose because the settlement calculated the fees based not on the size of the recovery for interest wrongfully withheld, but rather on the size of the underlying escrow accounts *in toto*, and it provided that the attorneys' fees would come from the escrow accounts rather than from the defendant. That resulted in some class members' accounts being credited with tiny recoveries (ranging from zero to $8.76) and being debited for attorneys' fees in far larger amounts ($91.33 for Kamilewicz). Thus, many class members emerged from the court-approved settlement worse off than they would have been if class counsel had gone to trial and lost. To make matters worse, the Alabama defendants had offered to settle and to pay attorneys' fees (of $500,000) out of the bank's own funds, which would have left the class members with the credits that their accounts deserved, paltry though they may have been. Class counsel had rejected the settlement.

This aggrieved some of the class members, who brought an action in Illinois federal court against the class action attorneys and some of the defend-

---

[253] Kamilewicz v. Bank of Boston Corp., 92 F.3d 506 (7th Cir.), *reh. en banc denied*, 100 F.3d 1348 (7th Cir. 1996).

ants from the Alabama action, alleging claims under RICO and common law claims for fraud, negligent misrepresentation, breach of fiduciary duty, and conversion. The Illinois defendants then had the plaintiffs served in the Alabama action with an order to show cause why the Alabama settlement was not binding. Plaintiffs appeared by counsel for the sole purpose of advising the court that they would not participate in the hearing because the Alabama court lacked personal jurisdiction over them. The Alabama court reaffirmed the settlement.

The Illinois federal court dismissed the action under FED. R. CIV. P. 12(b)(1) on the ground that *Rooker-Feldman* deprived it of jurisdiction because even the ostensibly independent common law claims were "inextricably intertwined" with the merits of the Alabama litigation, making the case an impermissible collateral attack on the Alabama judgment. On appeal, a Seventh Circuit panel affirmed.

> We ask whether the federal plaintiff seeks to set aside the state court judgment or whether he is, in fact, presenting an independent claim. Put another way, if the injury which the federal plaintiff alleges resulted from the state court judgment itself, then *Rooker-Feldman* controls, and the lower federal courts lack

> jurisdiction over the claim. It does not
> matter that the state court judgment
> might be erroneous or even unconstitu-
> tional. Nor does it matter that the time
> for appeal to the United States Supreme
> Court may have passed.

The plaintiffs unsuccessfully sought rehearing *en banc*, five Seventh Circuit judges dissenting from the denial. The plaintiffs were out of luck.

Nonetheless, Judge Easterbrook's dissent raised some thorny problems about *Rooker-Feldman*'s applicability. It argued that the attack on the Alabama court's jurisdiction by the unnamed class members was a permissible collateral attack. Neither the original notice to class members nor the notice of the proposed settlement advised class members that they were at risk for having to pay attorneys' fees out of their own pockets rather than as a component of the settlement recovery. (Contingency fees come out of amounts recovered, not out of plaintiffs' separate assets.) The dissenters said that if one or both of the notices to the unnamed class members were defective, then either (1) jurisdiction over those members never attached because the original notice did not satisfy the constitutional requirements of *Phillips Petroleum Co. v. Shutts*[254] or (2) jurisdiction failed when the notice

---

[254] 472 U.S. 797 (1985).

of settlement failed to advise the class members of their financial exposure. Either way, there was a due process violation. That meant that the Alabama "judgment" was no more entitled to full faith and credit than the Oregon state-court judgment had been in *Pennoyer v. Neff*. "[A] judgment that is not entitled to full faith and credit does not acquire extra force via the *Rooker-Feldman* doctrine."

The dissent also pointed out that were the majority's approach followed to its logical conclusion, no federal collateral attack on a state-court default judgment would ever be permissible, so that a defendant who defaulted in the state-court action because there was no basis for personal jurisdiction would not be able to resist enforcement proceedings brought in a federal court.

> Collateral attacks based on lack of personal or subject-matter jurisdiction are proper, no less in class actions than in other cases—indeed, they are especially appropriate where class members are stunned to find that, although aligned as plaintiffs, they are net losers, just as if the original defendants had filed and prevailed on a counterclaim of which they received no notice and over which the state court had no jurisdiction. In effect, though not in name, this was a defendant class, attempting (unbeknownst to its

> members) to fend off predatory lawyers'
> claims to the balances in the escrow ac-
> counts.   The substantial jurisdictional
> problems entailed by defendant classes,
> were aggravated by the class members'
> ignorance of their exposure.

That is a difficult argument to refute; perhaps it
was wise that the *en-banc* majority did not try.

So was *Kamilewicz* a forbidden appeal, a permissible or impermissible collateral attack, or an
independent action.   The formal answer—because
the *en-banc* majority had the votes—is that it was
an impermissible collateral attack.   Yet who had
the better of the argument?   The point is that there
may be no definite answer, but the panel's opinion
and the *en-banc* dissent demonstrate anew to us as
counsel the critical nature of characterization.

C. Standing

After having written a bad check, an individual
sent a money order in full payment.   A collection
agency thereafter began a state action on the bad
check.   Although the individual received notice of
the action, he defaulted, apparently in the layman's
belief that the money order settled the controversy.
The state court entered judgment against him and
refused to set it aside because the individual presented no proof of having a meritorious defense,
which state law made a prerequisite to opening a

default judgment. The individual brought a federal action seeking two things: (1) that the court set aside the default judgment, and (2) that the court declare the state requirement of a meritorious defense unconstitutional. The district court granted relief.[255]

The Tenth Circuit found that the district court lacked jurisdiction because of *Rooker-Feldman*. Although it is generally true that a request for generalized, forward-looking relief avoids *Rooker-Feldman* (as in *Feldman* and *Centifanti v. Nix*), in *Facio* there was a problem. The request that the federal court set aside the Utah judgment clearly ran afoul of *Rooker-Feldman*, so that part of the action could not go forward. Eliminating that request for relief, however, meant that Facio lacked standing to seek the declaratory judgment on the constitutionality of the Utah rules. Without being able to allege any harm that the rules had caused him, Facio could show no injury-in-fact; he had only speculation that he might, at some future time, be subject to the rules.[256]

---

[255] Facio v. Jones, 714 F. Supp. 504 (D. Utah 1989), *vacated and remanded for dismissal*, 929 F.2d 541 (10th Cir. 1991).

[256] *See, e.g.*, City of Los Angeles v. Lyons, 453 U.S. 1308 (1981).

Thus, the Tenth Circuit found that Facio's request for declaratory relief was "inextricably intertwined" with the question of the validity of the default judgment, and therefore not within the federal courts' subject-matter jurisdiction. What made *Feldman* and *Centifanti* different? Those cases are distinguishable because Feldman and Centifanti retained the right to apply for admission to the bar, so their requests for declaratory relief were not speculative. Utah procedure did not allow Facio to continue to seek to have the default judgment set aside.

VII. THE ELEVENTH AMENDMENT

The Framers, largely following the political theory of John Locke, viewed the people as the true sovereign, with government as the people's trustee under the Constitution. That is why the Preamble begins, "We the People." United States law, however, routinely treats both federal and state governments as sovereigns. The difference is important; were it not for the substitution the law has made, no institution of government could raise an immunity defense to a charge of having violated constitutional rights. As the law stands, individuals who have suffered constitutional violations often have no effective remedy either against the state or its officials.

The Eleventh Amendment[257] appears to be a forum immunity, merely insulating states from being defendants in diversity litigation. The Court has read it far more broadly than that, however, and it now forbids jurisdiction over federal-question actions by individuals against states, despite its distinctly diversity-sounding wording. In addition, the Court takes the position that state sovereign immunity from individuals' suits antedated the Con-

---

[257] The judicial power of the United States shall not be construed to extend to any suit in law or equity, commenced or prosecuted against one of the United States by citizens of another state, or by citizens or subjects of any foreign state.

189

stitution[258] and that the Amendment merely reflects that understanding.

A.   The General Principle—Individuals' Actions Against States[259]

Chisholm v. Georgia[260] allowed recovery to the estate of a citizen of South Carolina on a bond that Georgia issued during the revolution; the action sounded in diversity.   The states' reaction was swift.   Reasoning that the Amendment restores the original understanding of Article III, the Supreme Court has gone well beyond the Amendment's words to hold that the judicial power does not include a suit against a state in admiralty[261] or by a federal corporation.[262]   Most important, *Hans v. Louisiana*[263] disallowed an action against the state by one of its own citizens, even though it was a federal-question rather than diversity case.   *Hans* was

---

[258] States that entered the union after ratification of the Constitution enjoy the same degree of protection under the Equal Footing Doctrine, which recognizes that later-entering states enjoy all of the state sovereign prerogatives of the original thirteen.   Mayor of New Orleans v. United States, 35 U.S. (10 Pet.) 662 (1836).

[259] The Court has ruled that actions against state-level departments "count" for Eleventh Amendment purposes as actions against the states.

[260] 2 U.S. (2 Dall.) 419 (1793).

[261] Ex parte New York, 256 U.S. 490 (1911).

[262] Smith v. Reeves, 178 U.S. 436 (1900).

[263] 134 U.S. 1 (1890).

ambiguous about the ground for the decision; the Court, referring to Hans's argument that the Eleventh Amendment could not apply to his action because he was not a "citizen[ ] of another state," acknowledged that, "if there were no *other* reason or ground for abating his suit, it might be maintainable * * * ." (Emphasis added.) The Court never made clear what that other reason might have been. Subsequent decisions, however, read *Hans* as an Eleventh Amendment case. Similarly, though the Constitution is silent, the United States is implicitly immune from suit as well.[264]

Dictum in *Principality of Monaco v. Mississippi*[265] suggested that foreign states enjoyed a comparable constitutional immunity. But in 1976, Congress passed the Foreign Sovereign Immunities Act, purporting to make foreign states suable in actions "based upon a commercial activity" or a "tortious act or omission" with connections to the United States.[266] Thus Congress thought the *Monaco* foreign-state immunity was not of constitutional dimension. Yet the argument for a constitutional immunity is similar to that made in any suit

---

[264] Kansas v. United States, 204 U.S. 331 (1907). Substate governments (counties, cities, villages), which are municipal corporations, do not share the states' immunity. Chicot County v. Sherwood, 148 U.S. 529 (1893).

[265] 292 U.S. 313 (1934).

[266] 28 U.S.C. §§ 1604-05

against a government irrespective of the Eleventh Amendment. As Hamilton said in The Federalist to quiet fears that the Diversity Clause would make states subject to suit in federal court, "[i]t is inherent in the nature of sovereignty not to be amenable to the suit of an individual without its consent." In 1972, Congress applied the anti-discrimination requirements of the 1964 Civil Rights Act to employees of state governments and expressly authorized relief against states that violated its provisions. Numerous decisions had made the obvious point that Congress could not give federal courts jurisdiction of matters outside Article III's definition of the federal judicial power, and *Hans* established that individuals' actions against states did not fall within that Article. Nevertheless *Fitzpatrick v. Bitzer*[267] upheld the statute on the ground that Section 5 of the Fourteenth Amendment, expressly authorized Congress "to enforce, by appropriate legislation, the provisions of this article." Since the first section of that Amendment expressly embodies "limitations on state authority," the Court concluded the Fourteenth Amendment implicitly modified the preexisting doctrine of state sovereign immunity, and Congress could enforce it by "provid[ing] for private suits against States or state officials which are constitutionally impermissible in other contexts." The reasoning is less than overpowering. One might

---

[267] 427 U.S. 445 (1976).

have thought § 5 of the Fourteenth Amendment, like other grants of legislative power, was subject to explicit and implicit constitutional limitations. That the Amendment limits state sovereignty, moreover, does not distinguish it from the Impairments Clause, which the Court had long held limited by sovereign immunity.

Fitzpatrick did not hold that the Fourteenth Amendment itself negated state sovereign immunity; the decision rested on Congress's express abrogation under § 5. Thus, in the absence of statute, the state is immune even if the case rests upon the Fourteenth Amendment, and the Court has continued to hold that § 1983, which does not expressly authorize suits against states, does not lift their constitutional immunity because states and their officials acting in their official capacity are not "person[s]" within the meaning of § 1983.[268]

Sovereign immunity (especially against claims of constitutional violations) is not an attractive concept, but implicit constitutional immunities are as old as *McCulloch v. Maryland*.[269] If, as the Court has repeatedly held, sovereign immunity limits Article III's grants of judicial power, and intergovernmental immunity forbids Congress to co-opt state

---

[268] Will v. Michigan Dep't of State Police, 491 U.S. 58 (1989).

[269] 17 U.S. (4 Wheat.) 316 (1819).

legislative or executive agencies under the Commerce Clause,[270] it follows that immunity from suit also limits the Commerce Clause. Yet, the Court has held that state agencies defending adversary proceedings in bankruptcy cases do not have Eleventh-Amendment immunity.[271] The question remains, however, whether it is the Commerce Clause or the Bankruptcy Clause that is unique in this respect.

B. Waiver

The Amendment's wording makes it sound like a jurisdictional provision. One might expect, therefore, that states cannot consent to suits in the federal courts any more than other litigants can extend courts' subject-matter jurisdiction by consent. But it has not been consistently so. The Court allows states to raise the Eleventh-Amendment issue for the first time on appeal,[272] explaining "that the Eleventh Amendment defense sufficiently partakes of the nature of a jurisdictional bar so that it need not be raised in the trial court." In the same case, however, the Court noted that states can waive their immunity, but "only where stated 'by the most

---

[270] Printz v. United States, 521 U.S. 898 (1997); New York v. United States, 505 U.S. 144 (1992).

[271] Central Va. Community Coll. v. Katz, 546 U.S. 356 (2006).

[272] *E.g.*, Edelman v. Jordan, 415 U.S. 651 (1974).

express language or by such overwhelming implications from the test as (will) leave no room for any other reasonable construction.' " Thus, a state's mere participation in a federal funding program subject to extensive federal regulation does not subject the state to federal adjudication. The Court noted, rather icily, that "Constructive consent is not a doctrine commonly associated with the surrender of constitutional rights, and we see no place for it here."

For example, California's constitution provides: "Suits may be brought against the State in such manner and in such courts as shall be directed by law."[273] The Court held that language insufficiently specific that California was consenting to suit in a *federal* court and refused relief. But the Court has also unanimously held that a state's decision to remove or to join other defendants in removing a case *does* constitute waiver.[274] So one may legitimately ask whether the Amendment speaks to subject-matter jurisdiction or merely establishes an immunity. The Court's answer appears to be, "Yes."

---

[273] Atascadero State Hosp. v. Scanlon, 473 U.S. 234, 241 (1985).

[274] Lapides v. Bd. of Regents, 535 U.S. 613 (2002).

C. The Eleventh Amendment and State Officials

Governments, like corporations, can act only through agents; to enjoin a government official from acting effectively enjoins the government, and some nineteenth-century decisions extended states' Eleventh-Amendment protection to cases brought against state officials to enforce contracts with the state. Most involved states defaulting on bonds by declining to recognize or accept them as payments of taxes. The reasoning was that the official was simply a proxy defendant for the state, and the relief would have run against the state rather than against the official.

On the other hand, if sovereign immunity were a bar to all injunctions against government officers, enforcing constitutional restrictions on the exercise of government power would be almost impossible. Another line of nineteenth-century cases held that actions in the nature of tort against state officials on the ground that the officials had acted unconstitutionally were maintainable notwithstanding the Eleventh Amendment. The two lines of cases almost inevitably had to collide in a case where a state officer was enforcing a state law alleged to be unconstitutional.

Ex parte Young[275] was that collision, and the Court upheld federal jurisdiction, rejecting Young's claim of Eleventh-Amendment protection by declaring that when he violated the Constitution (something the state could never authorize), the violation stripped him of the Eleventh-Amendment protection he would otherwise have enjoyed. Nonetheless, his actions, possible only because the state had vested power in him, continued to be state action for purposes of the Fourteenth Amendment.[276] *Ex parte Young* was an action to prevent enforcement of a state rate statute alleged to be unconstitutionally confiscatory.

Two theories of stripping compete for attention in *Ex parte Young*. The supremacy-stripping language is clear, but there is also language in the opinion echoing the far older idea that "the King can do no wrong." That phrase originally meant the opposite of what many today think it means.

---

[275] 209 U.S. 123 (1908).

[276] Before the 1976 amendment to the Administrative Procedure Act explicitly authorizing similar actions against federal officials, the Court applied the same reasoning to them as well. Many commentators have characterized the juxtaposition of the official's Eleventh-Amendment non-immunity with the view that his actions are still under color of state law as "a fiction" or "judicial sophistry." Perhaps, but is it so unusual in the law to have a term mean one thing in one context and something else in a different context? One can, for example, be incompetent to stand trial on a criminal charge and at the same time be entirely competent to make a will or manage financial affairs.

The Crown was immune from suit unless it consented, but if an official violated the Crown's law, the act was unauthorized, which deprived the officer of the Crown's immunity. Thus, the defendant stood before the court as an individual, as subject to judgment as any other. Either stripping theory supports *Ex parte Young*'s result, but what about when the state official violates state law? The state has not authorized his action. Why should the official be entitled to the state government's immunity for protection against a charge of violating state law? It may make little sense, but the Court found that the official retained Eleventh-Amendment immunity against state-law claims although having lost it with respect to federal claims.[277]

But *Ex parte Young* does not inevitably expose a state officer to suit on the ground that she is acting beyond her authority. For example, *Edelman v. Jordan*[278] held that the Eleventh Amendment forbids federal courts to order a state officer to make welfare payments out of the state treasury to remedy past violations of federal law. Acknowledging that *Young* authorized injunctions against future violations, the Court invoked earlier decisions refusing to order tax collectors to pay refunds with public money, concluding that a private suit "seek-

---

[277] *See infra* at 184

[278] 415 U.S. 651 (1974).

ing to impose a liability which must be paid from public funds in the state treasury" for past wrongs did not come within *Ex parte Young*, which concerned only prospective relief.

There is little to recommend this distinction. In one of the tax cases *Edelman* cited, the Court had said the suit was "in essence" against the state and that the state was the "substantial party in interest," but that was equally true in *Ex parte Young*. As the Court has acknowledged, an injunction permissible under *Young* can have as great an impact upon state policy as the order *Edelman* rejected. Indeed, the *Edelman* Court affirmed the district court's order that in future state officials comply with federal timing requirements regarding processing welfare applications and paying benefits. That undoubtedly ended up costing the state more money than it would have had to pay for three years of past violations.

Nevertheless, *Edelman* accorded fully with precedent and was not a retreat from *Ex parte Young*. Reviewing a long series of prior cases, the Court divided suits against state officers into two categories. A suit to compel officers "to do acts which constitute a specific performance" of state contracts was forbidden; a suit to preclude "acts of wrong and injury to the rights and property of the plaintiff acquired under a contract" was not. Thus, immunity precluded a federal court from ordering a state auditor to pay the holder of bonds on which the state had defaulted, but it did not preclude a federal court injunction against seizing the bonds themselves.

The source of these unsatisfying distinctions was the rationale the Court used to permit suits for injunctive relief in such cases as *Ex parte Young*. As the Court had explained in earlier cases, if violating the Constitution strips a state officer of his identity as the state, then he cannot breach the state's contract; only the state is a party to the obligation. On the same reasoning, an officer stripped of his authority could not be responsible for failure to satisfy the state's welfare obligations in *Edelman*.

By the time of *Edelman*, the Court had lost sight of the original reason for these distinctions, and *Edelman* did not rely directly on the cases that made them. In later cases, the Court has taken a broader view of the relief available against a state officer. For example, *Hutto v. Finney*[279] upheld an award of attorneys' fees payable from state funds on the ground that Congress (in 42 U.S.C. § 1988) had abrogated the state's immunity under *Fitzpatrick v.*

---

[279] 437 U.S. 678 (1978). Since § 1988 does not mention states specifically, one might wonder whether the super-strong-clear-statement rule of Atascadero State Hosp. v. Scanlon, 473 U.S. 234 (1985), undermines this part of Hutto. To date, no court has so held.

Bitzer.[280] It also sustained an additional award not covered by that statute on the ground that it was "ancillary" to a prospective injunction and thus permissible under *Edelman*.

Milliken v. Bradley[281] is more significant. The Court upheld an order requiring state money to provide "compensatory or remedial educational programs for schoolchildren who have been subjected to past acts of *de jure* segregation." This order, the Court said, fit "squarely within the prospective-compliance exception reaffirmed in *Edelman*" because it required the state to set up the remedial program "prospectively." But all relief for past wrongs is prospective in that sense; the officer in *Edelman* had been ordered to pay past-due installments in the future. *Milliken* added that the money was not to go to the wronged pupils themselves, but it did not say why that mattered.

Pennhurst State School & Hospital v. Halderman,[282] stands in sharp contrast to the permissive attitude of *Edelman*, *Fitzpatrick*, and *Milliken*. It held that the Eleventh Amendment bars even prospective relief against a state official if the legal ba-

---

[280] Section 1988 does not, however, contain anything like the kind of explicit statement that *Atascadero* said was necessary.

[281] 433 U.S. 267 (1977).

[282] 465 U.S. 89 (1984).

sis for the relief is state rather than federal law, and that the bar exists not merely if the state official failed to implement state law, but even if he acts contrary to state law. The narrow majority read *Ex parte Young* to have allowed stripping only to enforce supremacy, a consideration not present when state law furnished the rights the plaintiffs claimed.

The bitter[283] dissent argued that this conclusion was a radical, unacknowledged departure from precedent, and that *Ex parte Young*'s underlying theory was that any officer acting without authority was not the "state" for immunity purposes. That theory was applicable by definition to officers acting contrary to federal or state law. *Pennhurst* demonstrates the importance of the stripping theory underlying *Ex parte Young*. If *Young* stands only for supremacy stripping, then *Pennhurst* is correct. If *Young* also recognizes king-can-do-no-wrong stripping, then the *Pennhurst* majority erred. *Young* itself is unclear, but supremacy stripping dominates modern thought.

One more limitation of *Ex parte Young* has appeared. The Indian Gaming Regulation Act (IGRA) mandated a multi-step negotiating procedure be-

---

[283] The opinions contained numerous, only thinly veiled, *ad hominem* attacks on their opposing authors with a stridency rarely seen.

tween Tribes and the states in which they lived if a Tribe wanted to establish a casino. One section of IGRA vested jurisdiction in federal courts in tribal actions against the state if the state either refused to negotiate or did not negotiate in good faith. *Seminole Tribe v. Florida*[284] held that jurisdictional section unconstitutional, distinguishing the *Fitzpatrick* line of cases on the ground that the Fourteenth Amendment came after the Eleventh and therefore could modify it, whereas the Indian Commerce Clause, under which Congress passed IGRA, preceded the Eleventh Amendment.

As an alternative, the Tribe sought to compel the state to negotiate under the remaining sections of IGRA, using *Ex parte Young*'s supremacy-stripping theory. A narrow majority ruled that *Ex-parte-Young* relief was unavailable, reasoning that Congress, having provided a comprehensive statutory scheme to enforce the rights IGRA created, implicitly disapproved relief under *Ex parte Young* because such relief might run beyond the remedies Congress had provided. The Court did not com-

---

[284] Seven years before *Seminole Tribe*, a fractured Court held that Congress could abrogate states' Eleventh-Amendment protection using its Commerce-Clause power. Pennsylvania v. Union Gas Co., 491 U.S. 1 (1989), *overruled by* Seminole Tribe v. Florida, 507 U.S. 44 (1996). There was no majority opinion. Justice White, the fifth vote for the result, though concurring in the judgment Justice Brennan's plurality opinion announced, said he could not subscribe its reasoning. He did not say how he reached the result.

ment either on the fact that the Tribe's *Ex-parte-Young* argument sought only the precise negotiating-scheme relief that Congress had authorized in IGRA or on the propriety of denying relief under *Ex parte Young* on the ground of a statutory scheme the majority had just declared unconstitutional.

VIII. OFFICIALS' IMMUNITIES

A. Absolute Immunity

There is a short list of beneficiaries of absolute immunity. The President, prosecutors, judges, witnesses, and legislators have absolute immunity. "Absolute immunity," however, is something of a misnomer, for it does not immunize its beneficiaries from all forms of judicial action. It applies to its beneficiaries only when they are acting in the capacities that entitled them to immunity, and it does not immunize them from equitable relief.

For example, when a prosecutor elects to file criminal charges and pursues them through the judicial process, she is absolutely immune for exercising her prosecutorial powers—even if the would-be plaintiff alleges bad faith in the prosecution.[285] On the other hand, if she steps out of her role as prosecutor, such as by directing the police to execute a *capias ad respondendum* in a manner that violates the Fourth Amendment, she has only a qualified immunity.[286] Similarly, a judge is ordinarily immune from civil liability for any judicial act,[287] but

---

[285] Imbler v. Pachtman, 424 U.S. 409 (1976).

[286] Pembaur v. City of Cincinnati, 475 U.S. 469 (1986).

[287] Stump v. Sparkman, 435 U.S. 349, 356-57 (1978). Even this immunity may not be absolutely absolute. "A judge will not be deprived of immunity because the action he took was in error, was done maliciously, or was in excess of his authority; rather, he will be subject to liability only when he has acted in the " 'clear absence of all jurisdiction.' " The Court noted that a

when a judge also supervised the court's probation officers and fired one because of her sex, the judge performed a non-judicial act and had only qualified immunity.[288] Neither prosecutors[289] nor judges[290] are immune from suits seeking injunctive relief.

Curiously, only two immunities find mention in the Constitution. Article I, § 6, cl. 1, protects Members of Congress from civil arrest (little seen nowadays) while attending a session or while traveling to or from it, though they are still subject to service of civil process. More significant, the Speech and Debate Clause of that section safeguards Members from most civil suits relating to them as officeholders. The purpose of this provision is to strengthen Congress's independence. All other absolute immunities come from the common law, but, because of the maxim that statutes in derogation of the common law get strict construction, Congress probably would have to be explicit to remove a common-law immunity.

---

criminal court judge trying a defendant for a nonexistent crime would be in excess of authority an immune. On the other hand, a probate judge with no subject matter jurisdiction other than decedents' estates who conducted a criminal trial would not be immune.

[288] Forrester v. White, 484 U.S. 219 (1988).

[289] Ex parte Young, 209 U.S. 123 (1908).

[290] Pulliam v. Allen, 466 U.S. 522 (1984).

B. Qualified Immunity

1. An Evolving Standard

The Court has also created a qualified immunity, which is a bit more slippery. Qualified immunity is a latecomer, making its first appearance by name in the Supreme Court in 1974.[291]

> [I]n varying scope, a qualified immunity is available to officers of the executive branch of government, the variation being dependent upon the scope of discretion and responsibilities of the office and all the circumstances as they reasonably appeared at the time of the action on which liability is sought to be based. It is the existence of reasonable grounds for the belief formed at the time and in light of all the circumstances, coupled with good-faith belief, that affords a basis for qualified immunity of executive officers for acts performed in the course of official conduct.

Thus, the Court described a sliding scale of executive immunity: the more discretion the officeholder had, the broader the immunity.

---

[291] Scheuer v. Rhodes, 416 U.S. 232 (1974). There were earlier cases that recognized what we today call qualified immunity.

Whether qualified immunity should rest on objective or subjective factors, or on a combination, vexed the Court for some time. In 1975, the Justices split, a majority ruling that both objective and subjective factors were relevant to qualified immunity in the context of a school-discipline case.

> The official himself must be acting sincerely and with a belief that he is doing right, but an act violating a student's constitutional rights can be no more justified by ignorance or disregard of settled, indisputable law on the part of one entrusted with supervision of students' daily lives than by the presence of actual malice.[292]

Justice Powell wrote for four Justices (concurring and dissenting). He agreed with the Court's result but complained about the *objective* part of the standard. "One need only look to the decisions of this Court—to our reversals, our recognition of evolving concepts, and our five-to-four splits—to recognize the hazard of even informed prophecy as to what are 'unquestioned constitutional rights.' "

Seven years later Justice Powell wrote for a strong majority in *Harlow v. Fitzgerald*,[293] restat-

---

[292] Wood v. Strickland, 420 U.S. 308, 321 (1975).
[293] 457 U.S. 800, 818 (1982).

ing the standard to exclude the *subjective* component of the standard. "Government officials per-
forming discretionary functions generally are
shielded from liability for civil damages insofar as
their conduct does not violate clearly established
statutory or constitutional rights of which a reasonable person would have known." He apparently
overcame his concern about the difficulty of ascer-
taining "unquestioned constitutional rights," but he
did not say how. More recently, *Ashcroft v. al-
Kidd*[294] reconfirmed the absence of any subjective
component to the standard, so allegations of a defendant's bad faith are unavailing.

2. Applying the standard

If an official seeks dismissal or summary judgment based on qualified immunity and the district
court rejects the request as a matter of law, the
qualified-immunity decision is final within the
meaning of 28 U.S.C. § 1291 and therefore eligible
for interlocutory appeal. Because a defendant may
seek such relief at several points in the litigation,
more than one interlocutory appeal is possible.
Ashcroft v. Iqbal[295] recognized that the range of issues considered issues of law for purposes of interlocutory appeal had expanded. Plaintiff argued
that the interlocutory appeal could address only

---

[294] 563 U.S. 1 (2011).

[295] 556 U.S. 662 (2009).

whether the complaint "avers a clearly established constitutional violation," not whether the pleading's factual allegations were otherwise sufficient under Rule 12(b)(6). The Court rejected the distinction, but also reaffirmed a case denying summary judgment on qualified-immunity grounds because the district court there had found a genuine issue of material fact. Fact-based inquiries are not suitable for interlocutory appeals.

Two kinds of questions arose after *Harlow*. The first concerned the sequence in which district courts should consider the issues. The second dealt with what is required to make a rule of law "clearly established."

a. Sequence of inquiry

Initially the Court ruled[296] that the district court should consider (1) whether the facts alleged showed a constitutional violation and (2) whether the right the plaintiff asserted was clearly established, in that order. Eight years later, *Pearson v. Callahan*[297] unanimously gave the district courts discretion to take the questions in whatever sequence offered the best prospect for early resolution. Many judges and commentators had been critical of the *Saucier* sequence as inviting binding

---

[296] Saucier v. Katz, 533 U.S. 194 (2001); Wilson v. Layne, 536 U.S. 603 (1999).

[297] 555 U.S. 233 (2009).

decisions in the nature of dicta on constitutional questions. Nonetheless, the Court recently reiterated the *Saucier*-sequence's utility, noting that it facilitates "development of constitutional precedent and is especially valuable with respect to questions that do not frequently arise * * * ."[298] If you find this difficult to square with the Court's normal reticence about non-dispositive constitutional adjudication, you are not alone.

The issue may have become less important. In *Camreta v. Greene*,[299] the district court granted summary judgment to the defendants both on grounds of qualified immunity and that the officials' actions were constitutional. The Ninth Circuit affirmed the judgment on qualified-immunity grounds after finding that the officials' actions were unconstitutional. The plaintiff did not appeal. The victorious officials, notwithstanding the circuit's final judgment in their favor, sought and received Supreme Court review. The Court, finding that the case before it had become moot, vacated the circuit's ruling on the constitutional issue despite the absence of a then-live controversy, explaining that the defendants had a continuing interest in the constitutional question because it might arise in later cases. Thus, although the lower courts may still

---

[298] Plumhoff v. Rickard, 134 S. Ct. 2012 (2014).

[299] 563 U.S. 692 (2011).

consider the constitutional issues first, there is less incentive for them to do so if qualified immunity will dispose of the case.

b. Clearly established?

The Court's view of what is clearly established for *Harlow* purposes has varied over time. Sometimes it is quite fact specific. When FBI agents invaded a home without a warrant, probable cause, or exigent circumstances to search for an absent fugitive, the Court overturned a ruling in favor of the plaintiff, explaining that just because the search violated the Fourth Amendment did not mean that it was objectively unreasonable within the meaning of *Harlow*.

> We have recognized that it is inevitable that law enforcement officials will in some cases reasonably but mistakenly conclude that probable cause is present, and we have indicated that in such cases those officials—like other officials who act in ways they reasonably believe to be lawful—should not be held personally liable. The same is true of their conclusions regarding exigent circumstances.[300]

Thus, the same search may be unreasonable for Fourth Amendment purposes but reasonable under

---

[300] Anderson v. Creighton, 483 U.S. 635, 641 (1987).

Harlow. The Court criticized the circuit court for considering the clearly-established question at too high a level of generality.

On the other hand, the Court subsequently ruled[301] that close factual identity is not necessary as long as the official conduct involved is clearly unlawful. It seemingly considered the case at a higher level of generality than *Anderson* had, drawing a dissent from *Anderson's* author and two other Justices.

---

[301] Hope v. Pelzer, 536 U.S. 730 (2002).

IX. CHOICE OF LAW IN
THE FEDERAL COURTS

A. Supremacy

The Supremacy Clause[302] is no more than a simple choice-of-law provision. To be sure, it is enormously important, but it is not difficult. The Clause says only that when there is a clash between federal law[303] and non-federal law, the federal law wins. The difficulties arise in deciding (1) upon interpreting competing sources of authority to determine whether there actually is an unavoidable clash, and (2) what to do when the clashes involve only state laws, where the Supremacy Clause does not help. That is the meat of the Conflict-of-Laws course.

B. The *Erie* Doctrine and Federal Common Law

1. The Source of the Problem

The difficulty that creates most choice-of-law problems in the United States, vertical and horizontal,[304] is inherent in having multiple, co-equal ju-

---

[302] U.S. CONST. art. VI, § 2.

[303] The Clause refers to "[t]his Constitution, and the Laws of the United States which shall be made in Pursuance thereof; and all Treaties made, or which shall be made, under the Authority of the United States * * * ."

[304] These terms refer respectively to the choice between state and federal law and to the choice among the laws of various states. Cases sometimes present both types of issues. *Erie R. Co. v. Tompkins*, 304 U.S. 64 (1938), did.

risdictions. Each state is the equal of each other state. The federal government and the state governments are co-equals also, despite the Supremacy Clause, because the Constitution makes some areas of law exclusively federal, some non-exclusively federal, and leaves all other matters exclusively to state law. One may think of Article I, § 8, as telling the federal government the areas in which it can act, but just as forcefully it tells the government by omission the areas in which it cannot act. Choice-of-law problems arise whenever there are co-equal authoritative sources of law.[305] When there is no method of choosing among competing laws, the system flounders. That is what happened under the Articles of Confederation, where there were frequent conflicts between state law and the law of the central government the Articles created. Bear in mind that the newly independent colonists tried out that model of national organization and discarded it in only six years because it worked so poorly. The Supremacy Clause was part of the answer to those difficulties.

2. *Swift v. Tyson*

The Supreme Court first attempted to deal with the vertical choice-of-law problem in *Swift v. Ty-*

---

[305] One might consider separation-of-powers issues as choice-of-law problems *within* a single government.

son.[306] At the outset, it confronted the Rules of Decision Act, § 34 of the Judiciary Act of 1789:[307]

> The laws of the several states, except where the constitution, treaties or statutes of the United States shall otherwise require or provide, shall be regarded as rules of decision in trials at common law in the courts of the United States in cases where they apply.

The difficult phrase was "laws of the several states," because it was unclear until *Swift* whether that included state common law as well as state constitutional or statutory law. *Swift*, an ordinary commercial law dispute, ruled that the phrase meant only the constitutions and statutes of the states and the limited amount of decisional law relating to real estate or other immovables. Otherwise, *Swift* declared, the federal courts were free to find and declare the common law as they saw it.

To the extent that the common law a state recognized and the common law the federal courts in that state recognized differed, *Swift* offered a forum-shopping opportunity that few astute lawyers could resist.[308] For cases that either state courts or

---

[306] 41 U.S. (16 Pet.) 1 (1842).

[307] The current version is 28 U.S.C. § 1652.

[308] It might have been unethical for them to have resisted. Do you see why?

federal courts could hear (usually diversity cases), counsel representing an out-of-state party might be able to choose whether a federal or state court would adjudicate. Counsel representing an out-of-state plaintiff would choose state or federal court depending on which viewed the common law more favorably to the client. The in-state defendant had nothing to say about the forum and so was stuck with whichever court plaintiff chose. Where the out-of-state party was the defendant, the in-state plaintiff could force the federal court to hear the case by filing there, but if plaintiff chose the state court, the out-of-state defendant could remove to the federal court if the common law was better there. The advantage to non-citizens of the state was clear, and a famous 1928 case[309] made it stand out in bold relief.

There were three Kentucky corporations—two taxi companies and the Louisville & Nashville Railroad (of *Mottley* fame). One of the taxi companies and the railroad wanted the taxi company to have exclusive rights to serve the Bowling Green station, but Kentucky common law forbade such exclusivity arrangements. Accordingly, the taxi company unincorporated in Kentucky, reincorporated in Tennessee, made the contract with the railroad, and sued the other taxi company and the railroad to

---

[309] Black & White Taxicab & Transfer Co. v. Brown & Yellow Taxicab & Transfer Co., 276 U.S. 518 (1928).

compel enforcement of the contract. You guessed it: the federal court's view of common law did permit exclusivity, so the plaintiff prevailed when it would clearly have lost in the Kentucky courts. The case was not unusual; only the attention it received was. To understand what was going on and what *Erie* changed, it is necessary briefly to recall the common law adjudication process that the colonists' English-law background exemplified.

3. The Jurisprudential Earthquake

At common law in England, judges did not conceive themselves to be making law at all; instead, they discovered it. For centuries, the dominant legal theory was that principles of law simply existed—a theory known today as natural law. The court hearing a case, rather than "making" law, would take a mental excursion among the extant legal principles, discover those that applied to the dispute, and "bring them back" to the courtroom to decide the case. For a common-law judge to "make" law would have been a usurpation and an unwarranted extension of judicial power. Thus, when natural-law theory was the order of the day, there were three sources of law in the United States: state law, federal law, and natural law.

In the late nineteenth century, the natural-law view began to fade. John Austin famously declared that "law is the command of the sovereign." That is the basic idea of legal positivism—that temporal law comes only from an authoritative human source. That idea strengthened, and Justice Holmes' dissent in the taxicab case eloquently urged its application in the United States:

> It is very hard to resist the impression that there is one august corpus, to understand which clearly is the only task of any Court concerned. If there were such a transcendental body of law outside of any particular State but obligatory within it unless and until changed by statute, the Courts of the United States might be right in using their independent judgment as to what it was. But there is no such body of law. The fallacy and illusion that I think exist consist in supposing that there is this outside thing to be found. Law is a word used with different meanings, but law in the sense in which courts speak of it today does not exist without some definite authority behind it. The common law so far as it is enforced in a State, whether called common law or not, is not the common law generally but the law of that State existing by the authority of that State without regard to what it may have been in England or anywhere else.

However eloquent, it was a dissent only, but it laid the foundation on which the Court, seven years after Holmes's departure, built *Erie*.

4. *Erie*

Erie was an ordinary negligence case. The accident occurred in Pennsylvania, but Tompkins filed a diversity action in New York (probably because the *Pennoyer-v.-Neff* bases for personal jurisdiction still reigned, and Erie was a New York corporation). The critical tort issue in the case was whether Tompkins, as he walked along a path paralleling the Erie tracks, was a licensee or a trespasser. Tompkins had won a judgment in the lower courts because the rule that the federal courts then followed under *Swift* made Tompkins a licensee, to whom the railroad owed a duty of reasonable care. Under Pennsylvania law, Tompkins was a trespasser and could not recover on the facts.

When the case reached the Supreme Court, Justice Brandeis and his colleagues surprised everyone by announcing that the issue was whether the Court should overrule *Swift*, a question no one had briefed or argued.[310] The first sentence announced that, "The question for decision is whether

---

[310] Tompkins, of course, would not have, and while the Court overruling *Swift* would have helped Erie in that particular case, as a general matter the *Swift* approach served large corporations well. Erie was no doubt more interested in the war than the battle.

the oft-challenged doctrine of *Swift v. Tyson* shall now be disapproved." That got everyone's attention.

The Court lost little time in saying that it was overruling *Swift*, and it advanced three reasons. First, new research made a persuasive case that *Swift* had misinterpreted "laws of the several states," that Congress had intended all along to include state common law. Of course, ninety-six years had passed, and although Congress had considered several bills over the years to overrule *Swift*, it never did correct the error, if error there was. The Court acknowledged that if only statutory interpretation were involved, it probably would not have overturned *Swift*. But, the Court said, "the unconstitutionality of the course pursued [by the federal courts] has now been made clear * * * ."

Second, Justice Brandeis observed that the *Swift* Court's hope that the decision would promote uniformity in state and federal interpretations of common law had not come to pass. "Persistence of state courts in their own opinions on questions of common law prevented uniformity * * * ." This, the Court observed, led to large-scale forum shopping to the detriment of in-state defendants, as had happened in the taxicab case. Thus, it made equal protection of the laws impossible.

You may wonder how, in light of the Supremacy Clause, the states were able to persist in their own opinions. The answer lies in the wording of the Clause and the reigning jurisprudential theory. Recall that the Clause speaks of "laws of the United States in pursuance" of the Constitution. The law that had developed under *Swift* was not federal law within the meaning of the Supremacy Clause—it was natural law—so the states were under no obligation to follow it. That led the Court to its third (and definitive) reason.

Under *Swift*, the federal courts had, for ninety-six years, been declaring rules of common law that Congress could not have enacted because they were outside of the areas of federal competence that (primarily) Article I, § 8, enumerated. This, the Court declared, was improper.

> Except in matters governed by the Federal Constitution or by acts of Congress, the law to be applied in any case is the law of the state. And whether the law of the state shall be declared by its Legislature in a statute or by its highest court in a decision is not a matter of federal concern. There is no federal general common law. Congress has no power to declare substantive rules of common law applicable in a state whether they be local in their nature or "general," be they commercial law or a part of the law of torts. And no clause in the Constitution

purports to confer such a power upon the federal courts.

This is the core of *Erie*, although the first sentence is a bit of an overstatement because there still is lots of federal common law, and it supersedes state law (by supremacy) when there is an unavoidable clash. The same day Justice Brandeis announced *Erie*, he also authored and announced the Court's decision in a case applying federal common law.[311]

The fourth sentence's mention of "substantive" law is the only appearance of that word in *Erie*, and "procedural" does not appear at all. Nonetheless, courts, scholars, and countless students have erected a mental dichotomy between substantive and procedural law, confusing those labels with analysis and assuming that if something is "substantive," state law applies and that if it is "procedural," federal law applies. That is often—but not always ("[A]ye, there's the rub"[312])—true. "Substantive" and "procedural" are simply labels that serve as shorthand for a choice-of-law decision reached after

---

[311] Hinderlider v. La Plata River & Cherry Creek Ditch Co., 304 U.S. 92 (1938) (which, by pure happenstance, is the case that immediately follows *Erie* in United States Reports, a coincidence that nonetheless reminds us that the *Erie* Court certainly recognized that federal common law continued to exist, having ruled out only federal *general* common (*i.e.* natural) law.)

[312] WILLIAM SHAKESPEARE, HAMLET, act. 3, sc. 1.

analysis. In addition, whether something is substantive or procedural may vary with the purpose of the question. Thus, statutes of limitation are "substantive" for vertical (*Erie*) choice-of-law purposes but generally "procedural" for horizontal (state-state) choice-of-law purposes.

Note what the Court accomplished in those few short sentences. First, it confirmed that common law was not a second-class citizen, somehow lesser in stature than statutes, although statutes can certainly change the common law. State law is state law, whether the legislature or the judiciary announces it. Second, the Court reaffirmed that Congress cannot pass laws outside its enumerated constitutional powers. Third, the federal courts have no broader power to create common law than Congress has to create statutory law; the branches' competence is coterminous.

Fourth, and most important, the Court fully adopted legal positivism. In declaring the non-existence of "federal general common law," the Court reduced from three to two the sources of law in the federal courts. Before *Erie*, there was state law, federal law, and general law. After *Erie*, general law at the federal level was gone.[313] If there is

---

[313] The states, of course, remain free to enact, derive or discover principles of law wherever they wish, subject only to the Constitution's limitations.

no federal competence in an area, state law governs *ex proprio vigore*—by its own force. The demise of federal general common law created a vacuum into which state common law flowed.

Justice Brandeis made clear that there was no problem with the Rules of Decision Act. The Court was declaring its own decision in *Swift* unconstitutional, a usurpation of powers reserved to the states. As he put it, "We *merely* declare that in applying the doctrine this Court and the lower courts have invaded rights which in our opinion are reserved by the Constitution to the several states."[314]

Justice Brandeis never did make entirely clear what constitutional provision the federal courts had so consistently violated. The opinion obliquely suggested the Tenth Amendment but did not cite it. The Court's emphasis on inequitable administration of the laws might be a reference to the Equal Protection Clause, except that appears in the Fourteenth Amendment and did not then apply to the federal government.[315] It might have been Article I, § 8, but the Court did not cite that either. So per-

---

[314] Emphasis added. Oh well, Justice Brandeis, if *all* you're saying is that the entire federal court system, following the Court's lead, had violated the Constitution for nigh unto to a century, then perhaps *Erie* isn't such a big deal after all.

[315] In *Bolling v. Sharpe*, a companion case to *Brown v. Board of Education*, the Court read an equal-protection component into the Fifth Amendment's Due Process clause, but that was sixteen years after *Erie*.

haps the point was that no part of the Constitution countenanced the power that the federal courts had exercised.

The federal courts were thenceforth to apply state law in areas where federal law could not constitutionally exist. But in cases touching more than one state, which state's laws? *Erie* demonstrates, but does not articulate, the answer. To understand the answer, consider the day-to-day problem *Erie* was trying to solve. The concern was vertical forum shopping—parties using diversity jurisdiction as a tool to be in state or federal courts according to which court used law more favorable to the party with the final say over choosing the forum. How does one eliminate that incentive for forum shopping? The answer is simple, but often misstated. The easiest way to banish the incentive to forum shop is to have both the state and federal courts use the same law to decide the merits of the case. That is where the misstatement causes a problem.

People are apt to remember that *Erie* said to apply the substantive law of the state in which the federal court sits. That is *almost* right. *Erie* really directs the federal court to apply the law that the state in which the court sits *would apply*. That is not always the substantive law of the state. Consider *Erie*. The accident happened in Pennsylvania, but the lawsuit was in New York. Nonetheless, *Erie* talked about Tompkins's status under Pennsylvania law. Why? The answer is that a New York state court would have applied Pennsylvania—not New York—law to determine Tompkins's status. The choice-of-law rule in tort cases at the time was *lex loci delictus*—the law of the place of the wrong. If the New York federal court should reach the same result that a New York state court would reach, then it should apply the same law.[316] The Court articulated that rule three years after *Erie*.[317]

When considering choice-of-law issues in a case—whether vertical or horizontal—keep firmly in mind that the inquiry goes issue by issue, so that the laws of different sovereigns may apply to different issues. This phenomenon is routine in diversity cases. By and large, the federal court in a diversity case will use state law to determine the merits of the case and the Federal Rules of Civil Procedure to decide procedural issues.[318]

---

[316] In conflict of laws, this is known as accepting the *renvoi*, which means that in applying state law, the federal court will apply the state's conflict-of-law approach to choice-of-law questions.

[317] Klaxon Co. v. Stentor Elec. Mfg. Co., 313 U.S. 487 (1941).

[318] *"Dépeçage"* denotes applying different sovereigns' laws to different issues in a case.

5. The Developing *Erie* Doctrine

Erie set out the basic approach, but it was an extreme case because the Court had ruled that the federal government had no power to prescribe the rule of tort law to govern Tompkins's status. What about cases when there is federal power? Such cases are more difficult, and the Court has approached the problems piecemeal and continues to struggle with them. There are two lines of cases to consider, one concerning laws other than the Federal Rules of Civil Procedure (the *Erie* line of cases) and the other concerning only the Federal Rules.

a. The *Erie* Line of Cases

(1) Statutes of Limitation and the Outcome-Determinative Approach

State law time-barred an equity action against a fiduciary.[319] The plaintiff sought to avoid the bar by arguing that in an equity case, the federal law of laches should govern timeliness. The Supreme Court ruled against her. There are three important aspects of the case. First, unlike in *Erie*, Congress certainly had the power to prescribe limitations periods for the federal courts. For that reason, the Court spoke of the *Erie* "policy" rather than the *Erie* constitutional imperative. Second, the Court characterized a federal court sitting in diversity as

---

[319] Guaranty Trust Co. v. York, 326 U.S. 99 (1945).

simply another court of the state. Third, the Court prescribed deciding whether something was "substantive" for *Erie* purposes by using an outcome-determinative approach. If the choice of state or federal law would decide the outcome of the case, then *Erie*'s policy required applying state law. The test itself has not survived intact, but the holding that state limitations law governs in diversity actions is still good.

(2) Demoting Outcome-Determinativeness

The outcome-determinative test quickly became a monster, dictating that state law governed even in situations where a Federal Rule of Civil Procedure was not only relevant, but directly on point. Had there been no adjustment, the Federal Rules of Civil Procedure would have become an endangered species in diversity cases.

The adjustment came in *Byrd v. Blue Ridge Electrical Cooperative, Inc.*,[320] a diversity workers'-compensation case from South Carolina. The vertical choice-of-law issue was whether the judge (under state law) or the jury (under federal practice) should decide whether the plaintiff was a statutory employee and thus without common-law claims. The Court demoted the outcome-determinative test to being only one factor of three that a federal court

---

[320] 356 U.S. 525 (1958).

should consider, the other two being (1) the strength of the state interest in having the state rule apply and (2) the strength of the federal interest in having federal law control. This balancing approach (*Byrd* balancing) recognized outcome-determinativeness as a non-dispositive weight on the state side of the balance. Justice Brennan's less-than-searching inquiry[321] turned up no strong state interest, whereas he identified federal control of the distribution of functions between judge and jury as a dominant federal interest.[322] It was almost as if the Supreme Court said to the states, "Under *Erie*, you can tell the federal courts what law to use to decide 'substantive' issues in diversity cases, but you cannot dictate which parts of the federal court system will perform that function."

---

[321] For example, he did not seem to consider that South Carolina might have wanted judges to decide to prevent juries overly sympathetic to plaintiffs from undermining the workers'-compensation system by being disinclined to find that plaintiffs were "statutory employees," entitled only to the limited remedy of workers' compensation.

[322] The Seventh Amendment did not clearly govern the case because workers' compensation actions were unknown in 1791, when the Seventh Amendment became part of the Constitution, and the Amendment speaks of "preserving" the right to jury trial. The Court found it unnecessary to address that question.

b. The Federal Rules of Civil Procedure

Congress passed the Rules Enabling Act (REA) in 1934,[323] authorizing the Supreme Court to promulgate procedural rules for the federal courts, subject to congressional rejection. Four years later, the FRCP came into effect. The statute contains a *proviso*: the rules could not "shall not abridge, enlarge or modify any substantive right." That is easily said but difficult of interpretation, as the Court's most recent Federal-Rules case[324] demonstrates.

The first case involving the Federal Rules reached the Court in 1941,[325] and a closely divided Court upheld Federal Rule 35 against an REA challenge, using the less-than-helpful test of whether the Rule "really regulates procedure,—the judicial process for enforcing rights and duties recognized by substantive law and for justly administering remedy and redress for disregard or infraction of them." The difficulty is that although the terms "substantive" and "procedural" fall trippingly from the tongue, their meaning is protean. *Sibbach* was on the right track, however, because at least it focused on REA.

---

[323] Current version at 28 U.S.C. § 2072.

[324] Shady Grove Orthopedic Assocs., P.A. v. Allstate Ins. Co., 559 U.S. 393 (2010). *See infra* at 225

[325] Sibbach v. Wilson & Co., 312 U.S. 1 (1941).

But when *Guaranty Trust* articulated the outcome-determinative test four years later, the Court seemed to lose its way. Although that case did not involve a Federal Rule of Civil Procedure, the Court began to use that test to resolve clashes between the FRCP and state law. That practice culminated in three 1949 cases. In each, a Federal Rule arguably applied (one clearly, by its own terms), and in each the Court ruled that the federal rule had to yield to the competing state rule because the choice between them, at that point in the litigation, was outcome determinative. The upshot seemed to be that the FRCP could apply in diversity cases only when they did not conflict with state law anyway. In one sense, the outcome-determinative test, when applied to the FRCP, turned supremacy on its head. None of the opinions in the three cases—including the dissents—so much as mentioned REA. All of the analysis occurred under *Erie* and *Guaranty Trust*.

The Court righted itself in *Hanna v. Plumer*.[326] State law mandated a more restrictive form of service of process than did Federal Rule 4. The choice between state and federal law would have been outcome-determinative. The Court nonetheless upheld the service made under Rule 4. The Court's opinion declared Rule 4 valid under REA, but *Han-*

---

[326] 380 U.S. 460 (1965).

na is important for far more than that. The Court declared that *Erie* (and *Guaranty Trust* and *Byrd*) exemplified the wrong approach to issues involving the FRCP.

> It is true that both the Enabling Act and the *Erie* rule say, roughly, that federal courts are to apply state "substantive" law and federal "procedural" law, but from that it need not follow that the tests are identical. For they were designed to control very different sorts of decisions. When a situation is covered by one of the Federal Rules, the question facing the court is a far cry from the typical, relatively unguided *Erie* Choice: the court has been instructed to apply the Federal Rule, and can refuse to do so only if the Advisory Committee, this Court, and Congress erred in their *prima facie* judgment that the Rule in question transgresses neither the terms of the Enabling Act nor constitutional restrictions.

Rule 4 applied because it spoke with "unmistakable clarity." That language is the initial source of the requirement that the Federal Rule be "directly on point" to govern.[327] Finally, the Court cautioned us

---

[327] Do not to make the mistake of applying the directly-on-point approach to interpreting a federal *statute* for *Erie* purpos-

to keep in mind what it characterized as the "twin aims of the *Erie* rule: discouragement of forum-shopping and avoidance of inequitable administration of the laws."[328]

Justice Harlan's concurrence offered a different (and better) perspective. In his view, the question should be whether the legal rule requiring a choice-of-law decision was "substantive" for *Erie* purposes if it affected "those primary decisions respecting human conduct which our constitutional system leaves to state regulation"—*i.e.* non-litigation conduct or conduct relevant to the merits of a claim or a defense.

6. The Past Half-Century

With *Hanna*, the methods for vertical choice-of-law analysis were in place. Everything since then has been application—not always easy application, to be sure—but until *Shady Grove*, the battles have been over application. Remember that when the nation began, there was only state law; the federal government had not yet come into being. Whenever there is a federal rule—"substantive" or "procedural"—it displaces state law that would otherwise

---

es. That approach is too narrow. The Court applies ordinary techniques of statutory interpretation to federal statutes. *See* Stewart Org., Inc. v. Ricoh Corp., 487 U.S. 22 (1988).

[328] With all respect to the Court, one really should call the "twin aims" the "twin *aim*" of *Erie*. Forum-shopping produced the inequitable administration of the laws.

govern. The Constitution, primarily in Article I, § 8, lists the areas in which federal law may displace state law. When federal law is within the Constitution (and, for the FRCP, within the limitations of REA), it displaces state law by supremacy. The question to ask, with respect to any vertical choice-of-law issue, is whether there is some dominant federal interest that justifies displacing state law that would otherwise govern.[329]

If there is a federal constitutional provision applicable, it displaces conflicting state law. Why? Supremacy. Similarly, if there is a constitutional federal statute, it displaces conflicting state law. Why? Supremacy. If there is a Federal Rule that is within the restriction of REA, it displaces conflicting[330] state law. Why? Supremacy.

Only if there is no provision of the Constitution, federal statute, FRCP (or some other federal regulation) to govern does one fall back on what *Hanna* called the "relatively unguided *Erie* Choice." Even there, the question is the same: whether there is

---

[329] I ask my students whether there is some BFD—Big Federal Deal—justifying displacement. It may lack the elegance of "dominant federal interest," but it seems to be more memorable.

[330] Here the requirement that the Federal Rule be "directly on point"—*i.e.* that it answer the precise question the issue poses—comes into play, but that requirement simply requires explicitness in the Federal Rules and disallows implication.

some dominant federal interest that justifies displacing state law. *Byrd* is an example. Although there was no federal law provision, the federal courts' interest in allocating adjudicative functions within the federal judiciary between court and jury was so important that it displaced the conflicting state rule. Even when the conflicting rules are substantive beyond question, federal law may nonetheless govern an issue in a diversity case, as it did when the federal and state applicable rules involved the conduct of foreign affairs.[331]

It turns out that characterizing a particular rule or law as substantive or procedural is quite unnecessary. The question is always whether there is some dominant federal interest that displaces state law. In the context of the *Erie* doctrine, the labels "substantive" and "procedural" are no more than conclusions based on the dominant-federal-interest analysis.

7. *Shady Grove*, the FRCP, and REA

New York law created a penalty for insurers who paid medical reimbursement claims late. It also forbade class actions in cases to recover penalties. A medical group brought a diversity class action to recover the owed penalty amounts, and the

---

[331] Banco Nacional de Cuba v. Sabbatino, 376 U.S. 398 (1964) (applying the federal act-of-state doctrine to a commercial dispute between the Cuban government and a corporation.

Supreme Court had to decide whether the action
was maintainable as a class action. That, in turn,
required the Court to consider whether the state
prohibition of class actions meant that applying
Rule 23 would cause the Rule to violate REA's
command that the Federal Rules not affect substantive rights. The Court split two ways, one on
the result and one on the proper method of analysis.
A five-to-four majority held the action maintainable, but there was no majority opinion for the result.

The result is not the important part of the case
for Federal Courts purposes; the method is. Four
Justices thought that to assess whether a federal
rule trenched on substantive matters the Court
should look only at the text of the federal rule. Five
Justices thought that one must also consider substantive policies that might underlie the conflicting
state "procedural" rule. Of those five, four thought
the state rule forbidding class actions in penalty
cases served a substantive purpose and so would
have interpreted Rule 23 to avoid the conflict. The
fifth Justice, though agreeing on the analytical
method, declined to find a substantive purpose in
the state rule. Thus, five Justices did agree on the
method, though they differed on the analysis applying the method in *Shady Grove*.

The majority approach—searching for state
substantive policies inherent in the state rule—is

more amorphous than the minority approach and therefore will be more difficult to apply. It is relatively easy to tell whether a Federal Rule directly addresses an element of a claim or a defense. It is much more challenging to discern an unspoken substantive policy in some state enactment that does not explicitly declare one, particularly if the enactment is in the state's procedural law, as it was in *Shady Grove*. Nonetheless, that is the inquiry that the Court has bequeathed us.

8. Federal Common Law

Notwithstanding the common misperception of what *Erie* said, federal common law continues to exist. The federal courts create it whenever there is some dominant federal interest that written federal law does not address. It is critically important to understand that some of that federal common law comes from federal cases that the federal courts decided during *Swift*'s reign.

In the years following *Swift*, the federal courts created lots of law. Only some of it was general law—law in areas that the Constitution authorized no federal power. The rest of it was genuine federal common law, for which there was a constitutional "hook," and, as federal law, was entitled to supremacy recognition in the state courts, unlike "federal general common law." There was no constitutional impediment either before or after *Erie* to such law, so do not be surprised (or, worse, have a knee-jerk reaction of invalidity) when you see modern cases using principles that courts following *Swift* articulated.

That is only one possible source of federal common law. Sometimes the courts look to model codes for ideas. On occasion the courts will adopt the common law of the state in which they sit as federal common law, preferring uniformity among all the courts that sit in that state to uniformity across the federal courts that may clash undesirably with the law of the state in which a federal court sits.

Judge Henry Friendly of the Second Circuit identified four methods that the federal courts use in creating common law: (1) spontaneous generation, (2) construing a jurisdictional grant as a congressional command to create common law, (3) implying private rights of action in constitutional or statutory provisions that confer rights, and (4) the ordinary judicial filling in of statutory interstices.

a. Spontaneous Generation

In 1943, the Court considered whether state or federal law should control whether delay in notification of forgery of a federally issued check barred recovery from a prior endorser automatically or only if the prior endorser could show prejudice from the delay.[332] The Court noted that *Erie* did not require applying state law because the federal government did have constitutional authority to issue checks, whereas in *Erie* it lacked the power to create rules of tort and property law. Reciting the great federal interest in the uniformity of law governing federally issued paper, the Court held that federal law would govern, and it applied a federal common law rule that it had announced before *Erie*.

b. Construing a Jurisdictional Grant as a Command to Create Federal Common Law

From the nation's beginning, the federal courts construed grants of jurisdiction as implicit congressional commands to create federal common law. The most prominent areas are admiralty and suits between states. It would have been impracticable to use state law, but Congress furnished no substantive law to speak of in either area.[333] More recently, the Court has gone beyond those areas.

Textile Workers Union v. Lincoln Mills[334] is the leading case. The Court ruled that Congress, by conferring jurisdiction on the district courts in cases

---

[332] Clearfield Trust Co. v. United States, 318 U.S. 363, *amended* 318 U.S. 744 (1943).

[333] A few statutes now exist governing small parts of admiralty law, but it remains largely federal common law.

[334] 353 U.S. 448 (1957).

involving labor-management disputes, intended as well that the federal courts create a federal common law of labor-management relations. One may gauge the strength of that inference by the Court's declaration that, "[t]he legislative history of § 301 is somewhat cloudy and confusing. But there are a few shafts of light that illuminate our problem."[335] The underlying dispute sounded in contract, ordinarily an area of state rather than federal power. That would have made federal-question jurisdiction impossible, but by construing the jurisdictional grant as it did, the Court then was then able to create federal common law. Conveniently, it found that the case arose under the federal common law it had just created.

Justice Frankfurter filed an extended dissent, disagreeing with the majority's interpretation of § 301. More than that, he declared that if the majority's interpretation of § 301 were correct, the statute would be unconstitutional, exceeding the limitations on the federal judicial power that Art. III, § 2, sets out. He did not dispute that Congress could create a federal law of labor-management relations under the Commerce Clause, but he had grave separation-of-powers misgivings that Congress could transfer that function to the judiciary.

---

[335] That is judge-speak that means, "It's there if we have the votes to say that it is."

Despite Justice Frankfurter's anguish, the Court has remained true to *Lincoln Mills*, though it rarely takes such a view of jurisdictional grants. Fifteen years after *Lincoln Mills*, the Court unanimously construed an environmental statute similarly to authorize creating federal common law,[336] and later followed the same path with respect to the Employee Retirement and Income Security Act.[337] The federal courts have also created a vast reservoir of antitrust law under the Sherman Act's extraordinarily broad, non-specific disapproval of contracts and combinations in restraint of trade.[338]

c. Implying Private Rights of Action in Constitutional or Statutory Provisions That Confer Substantive Rights

(1) In Constitutional Provisions

For many years, courts routinely recognized causes of action in statutes that created substantive rights, and Congress never disapproved the practice. Early cases spoke of "inferring" private rights of action,[339] but more recently the Court has char-

---

[336] Illinois v. City of Milwaukee, 406 U.S. 91 (1972).

[337] *See* Franchise Tax Bd. v. Constr. Laborers Vacation Trust, 461 U.S. 1, 24 n.26 (1983).

[338] *See* National Soc'y of Prof'l Eng'rs v. United States, 435 U.S. 679 (1978).

[339] *See, e.g.* Texas & P. Ry. Co. v. Rigsby, 241 U.S. 33, 39 (1916).

acterized the process as "implying" private rights of action. The difference is important from a separation-of-powers perspective. If the courts are inferring private rights of action, they are reading the underlying substantive provision to contain, albeit not explicitly, a private right of action. If the courts are implying private rights of action, they become the active parties, themselves creating the right of action rather than concluding that the statute or the Constitution already contains it.

In 1971, the Court recognized a Fourth-Amendment private right of action against federal law enforcement officials.[340] Justice Brennan's cryptic majority opinion did not clearly identify the source of the right of action. Justice Harlan's concurrence was a far better opinion.

Later, the Court also recognized private rights of action in the Fifth[341] and Eighth Amendments.[342] The constitutional well appears to have dried up, however, as subsequent Courts declined to find private rights of action in the First Amendment[343] and the Fifth Amendment's Due Process Clause (implicitly repudiating the earlier Fifth-Amendment

---

[340] Bivens v. Six Unknown Named Agents, 403 U.S. 388 (1971). Section 1983 creates a right of action but did not apply because the defendants were federal rather than state actors.

[341] Davis v. Passman, 442 U.S. 228 (1979).

[342] Carlson v. Green, 446 U.S. 14 (1980).

[343] Bush v. Lucas, 462 U.S. 367 (1983).

case).[344] The line that may connect the constitutional implied-right cases may be Justice Brennan's mention in *Bivens* that the Court would imply a private right of action unless there are "special factors counseling hesitation in the absence of affirmative action by Congress." Justice Brennan mentioned that federal fiscal policy might be such a factor.

The question today is what constitutes "special factors." Since *Carlson*, the Court has identified the following special factors as precluding *Bivens* remedies in constitutional cases: (1) the dispute involved servicemen's or former servicemen's allegations of constitutional violations by the military related to their service, (2) the existence of what the Court describes as a "comprehensive" congressional remedial scheme affording relief,[345] and (3) the dispute involved a non-military federal employment relationship, with Congress having provided limited administrative remedies. The chances of the Court implying a private right of action in a constitutional pro-

---

[344] Schweiker v. Chilicky, 487 U.S. 412 (1987).

[345] In *Chilicky*, the Court relied on this ground in refusing to allow a private right of action even though the Court acknowledged that the remedy was incomplete and the victims' suffering was "beyond what anyone of normal sensibilities would wish to see imposed on innocent disabled citizens." Query whether Congress thus appropriately limits remedies for *constitutional* violations. Could Congress limit *Bivens* damages to $1.00?

vision are substantially less than they were immediately after *Carlson*.

(2) In Federal Statutes

Implying private rights of action in statutes
was an accepted in England as early as 1703 and in
the United States at least from 1916 forward. It
reached its broadest sweep in *J.I. Case Company v.
Borak*[346] when a unanimous Court allowed a private right of action to rescind a corporate merger
alleged to have been effected because of a mislead-
ing proxy statement. The Securities Exchange Act
allowed enforcement only by the Securities Exchange Commission, but the Court found a private
action necessary to achieve Congress's purpose.

A decade later, the Court began to limit itself in
statutory implied-right cases. *Cort v. Ash*[347] unanimously prescribed a four-factor inquiry in place of
Borak's more free-wheeling approach: (1) whether
plaintiff was one of the statute's intended class of
beneficiaries, (2) whether the Court could discern
congressional intent either to create or to deny a
private right of action, (3) whether implying a private right of action was consistent with the legislative scheme, and (4) whether the dispute sounded
traditionally in federal or state law. Thus, *Borak*

---

[346] 377 U.S. 426 (1964).
[347] 422 U.S. 66 (1975).

shrank to being only one consideration of four. *Cort* declined to imply a private right of action in a federal criminal statute, in no small part because there was no identifiable class of intended beneficiaries smaller than all of society.

Under the *Cort* inquiry, implied private rights of action were still possible. Over Justice Powell's powerful dissent, the Court, implied a private right of action in Title IX of the Civil Rights Act of 1964 in favor of an applicant to medical school who alleged sex discrimination underlying her rejection. Justice Powell asked why, if Congress's purpose to benefit the class and allow a private right of action was as clear as the majority found, the statute did not contain one. The majority answered that Congress, when it passed Title IX, knew that the courts had implied a private right of action in Title VI and assumed that Title IX would receive the same treatment.

However, Justice Powell had raised an important separation-of-powers argument. He asserted that if Congress really wanted there to be private enforcement, it had only to include it in the statute. The fact that the courts had long stepped into the void did not impress him; repetition does not establish validity.[348]

---

[348] He also accused the majority of improperly expanding the federal courts' jurisdiction by taking in cases under implied

Cort's approach did not last long. Only four years later, a sharply split Court stepped back from it, declaring that "what ultimately must be determined is whether Congress intended to create the private remedy * * * ."[349] The Investment Advisers Act made certain contracts void if resting on fraudulent practices. The majority allowed a private right of action for rescission and restitution, common consequences of voidness, but it declined to imply a private right of action for damages. It recharacterized *Cort* factors 1, 3, and 4 as guidelines to congressional intent (factor 2) and nothing more. Although the Court has not embraced Justice Scalia's declaration that "we should get out of the business of implied private rights of action altogether,"[350] it will be the rare case that supplies a statutory private right of action that, in Justice Powell's terms, Congress "absentmindedly" forgot to include.

d. Filling in Statutory Interstices

No legislature can enact legislation that answers all of the questions that may arise concerning the subject of the statute. One might view the Internal Revenue Code, with its thousands of sections, regulations, revenue rulings, private letter

---

rights of action that Congress never intended the courts to hear.

[349] Transamerica Mortgage Advisors, Inc. (TAMA) v. Lewis, 444 U.S. 11 (1979).

[350] Thompson v. Thompson, 484 U.S. 174 (1988) (Scalia, J., concurring in the judgment).

rulings, generic legal advice memoranda (GLAMs), and general counsel memoranda (GCMs), as a joint attempt by Congress and IRS to answer all the questions. And yet, there still are thousands of cases each year requiring judicial interpretation of this mountain of material.

The practice of determining limitation periods for federal claims where the statutes creating the claims contained none is the best concrete example of this phenomenon.[351] Many statutes that explicitly created private rights of action, such as the Civil Rights Act of 1871,[352] expressed no limitation period. That left the courts with three possible inferences: (1) that Congress intended that there be no limitation period, (2) that Congress intended the federal courts to borrow some analogous limitation period from state law, or (3) that Congress intended the courts to create a limitation period. At different times, the Justices have used each approach. The cases adopting one approach or another are still good law, although Congress addressed the limitation problem in 1990, enacting 28 U.S.C. § 1658, which creates a four-year period for claims Congress creates after that date but leaves earlier, judicially prescribed periods untouched.

---

[351] Of course, statutes in which the Court implied private rights of action contained no limitation periods either.

[352] 42 U.S.C. § 1983.

Nutshell Series

- A succinct exposition of the law to which a student or lawyer can turn for reliable guidance.

- All titles written by outstanding authorities and recognized experts.

- A compact format for convenient reference.

WEST ACADEMIC
ISBN 978-1-63460-278-5

9 781634 602785

90000